£2.50

CHINESE ANIMAL SYMBOLISMS

CHINESE ANIMAL SYMBOLISMS

Ong Hean-Tatt

Author of *The Chinese Pakua*

Pelanduk
Publications

Published by
Pelanduk Publications (M) Sdn Bhd
24 Jalan 20/16A, 46300 Petaling Jaya
Selangor Darul Ehsan
Malaysia.

Perpustakaan Negara Malaysia
Cataloguing-In-Publication Data
Onn, Hean-Tatt
Chinese Animal Symbolisms/Ong Hean-Tatt
Bibliography: p.295–298
ISBN 967 978 435 5
1. Animals – Symbolic aspects.
2. Symbolisms.
I. Title.
306.4089951

Printed by
Eagle Trading Sdn Bhd
81 Jalan SS25/32, 47301 Petaling Jaya
Selangor Darul Ehsan
Malaysia.

PREFACE

Like other ancient cultures, the Chinese culture has a wide, seemingly bewildering range of delightful animal symbolisms. These symbols have been with the Chinese for centuries and every facet of their life and community living finds some association, whether remote or directly, in connection with these animal symbols.

The Chinese civilization has the longest historical continuity dating as far back as 2900BC. Much of the meaning of the animal symbolisms have persisted through many battles and dynasties and often found to have mystical magical roots. Time has changed some of the original interpretations and reasons for the symbolisms. It takes great pains to rediscover their true meanings and significance.

The present book is a comprehensive collation of the numerous references on the animal symbolism scattered through several literatures. It presents an analytical approach to the seemingly confusing mass of information, including some comparisons to animal symbolism in other cultures in order to gain an in-depth perspective of the ancient reasons for their existence.

This study is done through the eye of the Chinese Ganzhi System. This System is the foundation of the Chinese chronology, astrology and the geomantric art of *Feng-Shui*, and is also the fundamental basis for the Chinese animal symbolisms.

It is hoped that the reader would not only enjoy knowing what Chinese animal symbolisms truly signify but also absorb the positive Chinese philosophies underlying them. Chinese culture is one of gentle, light, refreshing positiveness and encouragement and the destined triumph of good over everything else.

The Chinese animal symbolisms may be surmised :
"Good fortune in the Lung-Phoenix."

CONTENTS

List of Tables

List of Illustrations

Figure

1

UNIVERSAL MEANINGS OF SYMBOLISMS

The number of images of gods it is impossible to tell completely, for the image of every god or demigod or hero accepted by mankind were carried there. Some were gilded and others adorned with gold-embroidered robes, and the myths belonging to each, according to accepted tradition, were represented by the most costly symbols. – *Polybius, describing the international games Antiochus Epiphanes instituted at Daphne, 165*BC.

Chinese culture has a rich variety of symbols. They represent mastery over everyday life, and portray a purposeful foray into the enchanting world of imagination. Chavannes (1973, p.17) comments that in China the decorations on articles of daily use are usually symbolic; they express good wishes. Their meanings could be hidden and need to be deciphered to help understand the reasons for the existence of the designs.

MacKenzie (1926) regards ancient symbols in various cultures as more than mere art or decorative motifs. Ancient symbols are not merely "art for art's sake" but sombre "luck motifs" or magico-religious motifs. Their significance was inspired by events rooted in ancient times and their true meanings lost and masked through the passage of time.

Symbols have meanings beyond visible forms and their shorthand lead to in-depth comprehension. They give us glimpses into the mentality of people who lived for millenniums under different skies (Hummel in Chavannes, 1973, p.9).

That shadow play in the world of imagination and dreams is not necessarily unreal. The Chinese philosopher Chuang-

Tzu once dreamt he was a butterfly and exclaimed on waking whether he, the man, or he, the butterfly, was the real being. It is the reality of that entity that scientists often dub as the unconscious, subconscious and even super-conscious. Psychologists and psycho-analysts realize that these imaginary worlds have reality which has profound effect on the everyday living of the person.

Carl Jung, the eminent modern psychologist, knew that some of these hidden levels of consciousness might be of higher levels; including that which the mystics called God, Brahman or Atman – that Super-Unconscious who communicates with Man in shadowy symbols.

On the sombre side, everyone at some time in life has encountered dark moments when life seems gripped in a fearful paralysed uncertainty. During such periods of remorse or despair, man seeks answers and hope from the supernatural powers which rest somewhere in the great unknown. These seekers look for omens which portend the will of the supernatural.

Ancient Chinese culture has assimilated a rich storehouse of these symbols of ancient roots. Each aspect of life is represented by a suitable collection of symbols – for the living, at birth and unto the dead. Much of the Chinese symbolism is very old. How do they persist through time? Waterbury (1952, p.139) notes that though the Bird-deities were not worshipped they were cherished for over fifteen hundred years.

SYMBOLS IN EVERYDAY LIFE

Symbolism is an essential universal characteristic of all religious cultures. Civilization depends on man's ability to use and invent symbols; language *per se* is a collection of an array of symbols manipulated to convey ideas. Without naming it, the idea cannot be expressed; the name is a symbol. It is necessary to use symbols to name a thing otherwise thoughts cannot go further. Human communication depends on symbolisms.

Initially pictorial symbolisms originated in the rituals of ancient worship, and preceded the written languages which, in their primeval forms, were pictorial. (Buttrick, 1954). Symbols were used to convey ideas and meanings and combined to coin new expressions. It was the ancient pictorial symbolisms which eventually gave rise to the alphabetical scripts.

Modern man could not escape the obvious use of symbolisms in modern communications. Traffic signs and direction signs guide a person through the cities, buildings and countryside. Symbols such as "No Entry" or "No Smoking" threaten violators. Symbols depicting danger could be ignored at one's own peril. Bright neon-light symbols from afar attract attention. Uniforms differentiate ranks and categories of people. The *macho* image and the *hip* image have their distinguishing styles of dressing. Fashions are symbolical in nature. Symbolism, thus, permeates the heart and throb of human society.

SIGNATURE-SEALS SYMBOLISM

An important everyday life binding symbolism used by modern man is his signature. By appending his signature to a document, the man signifies his acceptance of the contents of the document and seals the legal contract within. The signature binds him to honour the contents of the document.

In countries like China and Japan, the carved signature-seal, used for stamping documents, is still an accepted form of signature. Ancient orientals used decorative signature-seal chops for their signatures.

In agreements between nations, the signatures often have to be confirmed by the mark of the national seals. Various national seals have different symbols which characterize the authority of the different nations. These seals provide irrefutable evidence of agreements and therefore form the basis of legal contracts which must be honoured by all signing parties.

Symbolism is a living thing. Symbolism has taken on new shapes and usage. From the dawn of civilization to the contemporary era, symbolisms form essential parts of everyday living.

THE WAY OF MYSTIC SYMBOLS

The word "symbol" means standing for, representing or denoting something else. An "emblem" is something put on and is a symbol, though a symbol is not always an emblem. Symbols could be grouped as follows:

1. **Analogous** – representing an idea by something which suggests the idea.
2. **Associative** – representing an idea by an object associated with it.
3. **Imitative** – a part of the object to represent the whole.
4. **Indicative** – symbolizing an idea by the relationship of two or more things.
5. **Pictorial** – symbolizing by shapes within designs which suggest the object or idea.

Symbols form essential parts of ancient communications, especially at a time when alphabetical writings were not yet invented. However, one could not help wondering about the myriad of symbols in religious cultures and wonder what are really superfluous and what are really meaningful.

In the worship and magical rites of the religious cultures, many forms of symbols purport to exert mysterious powers on people. They are magic. How could the pasting of a religious paper symbol onto the door lintel ward off evil? If a black cat crosses one's path how could it bring evil to you? Religious symbols are therefore more than the kind of necessary symbolism modern man is familiar with. Religious symbols, especially those in charms and talismans, are attributed to some real forms of supernatural properties which could influence one's life.

SYMBOLS WITH SYMPATHETIC MAGIC

It is difficult to explain to the materialistic mind the element of the mystical and magical usage of religious symbols. There are some bases of how religious symbols purporting to have supernatural properties could work, namely:

1. Many symbols are sympathetic magic. They often include positive symbols like good luck signs, get-well signs. Such sympathetic magic stimulates the positive thinking in the person. The closer the symbol could be associated with the positive aspects the more likely the symbol would affect its purported power through stimulating the unconscious mind of the person. A form of this is the significance of names. Some people live up to what their names signify!

2. Some symbols pertain to unusual happenings. Animals exhibit certain behavioural patterns when earthquakes and storms are approaching. The ancients had studied such phenomena and attributed them to signalling the coming of good or bad fortunes. It is a science which modern scientists keen on forecasting earthquakes and storms, are beginning to probe.

3. Related to the above is the natural behaviour of animals or even plant life forms. Think of a dove and one gets a picture of innocence, peace and gentleness. Think of a lion and one gets a picture of fierce strength. Such images would definitely cause waves

in one's thoughts. If you imagine you were a lion you
would walk tall and brave. If you think you were a cur
you would certainly feel like one. Zodiacal images
may work at least through such auto-suggestive connections.

Some of the reasons above have psychological significance where the human unconscious mind harbours symbols which may seem innocuous but which have profound
effects on the person's mentality. Such symbolisms in the
deep recesses of the human mind play prominent roles in
psychoanalysis.

SYMBOLS USED IN SUMMONING SPIRITS

But in the end, there is still the esoteric magical reason for
symbols. One could never obtain a full understanding of the
power of symbols unless one admits the existence of a
psychic or spiritual dimension. Although there are sufficient
evidence of psychic and unusual supranormal phenomena,
many modern so-called educated people are reluctant to con-
cede to the reality of a spiritual dimension. To them, the magical use of symbols is nonsensical and they miss out the
significant ancient use of symbols.

Religious symbols also work because they have inherent
powers to summon and command the spirits. Practitioners of
religious magic realize that symbols regulate the spirits because many of these symbols are analogous to our signatures.
Symbols on talismans and charms are often the signature-
seals of powerful spiritual beings, or even God. Usage of
these signature-seals bound the representative powers to intervene and warn other spirits to meddle at their own peril and
having to answer to superior spiritual forces.

Spirits, like man, have pets and mascots. This is another way how certain animals would portend the coming of good or evil. It is one basis of animal symbolism in ancient cultures.

Some symbols do have magical powers.

GANZHI SYSTEM OF ANIMAL SYMBOLISMS

Think Chinese and one would invariably conjure up a myriad of delightful Chinese things. Chinese culture exudes and reflects light — the soothing aquamarine blue porcelains, the gentle and peaceful art of Chinese brush paintings, the soft, richly embroidered Chinese silk, the tasty dainty Chinese food dishes, the profound ancient philosophies and the polite race, where *giving face* is the most important facet of life. Chinese culture is very rich in symbolisms which inclines towards the sublime, the mysterious and the beautiful.

Among the Chinese symbolisms, animal symbolism, including birds and fishes, is of priority to the traditional Chinese. Animal designs, often in pairs, are prominent among the decorative art of the Shang and early Western Zhou bronzes which reached to its height during the An-Yang phase of the Shang period (Chang, 1983, p.56).

Animal symbolisms are most manifested in the philosophy of the Zodiacal Animals where it could influence marriage partnerships and affect important dates and ventures. But the Chinese bestiary has other forms of auspiciousness. There are various reasons why the Chinese put animal images everywhere around them – in temples, buildings, gardens and roadways, onto their furniture and utensils, and even onto their dresses and bedclothes. The animals are featured in their festivals and arts, and included in stories which are an everlasting delight to both the young and old.

The Chinese rich usage of animal symbolisms denotes the culmination of age-old observations on the animal world.

Thereby, using their distinct qualities and behaviour through symbols. The variety of animals featured in ritualistic worship among ancient cultures is formidable.

These animals include the following: Alligator, anteater, ape, armadillo, ass, baboon, bat, bear, beaver, bison, boar, buffalo, bull, camel, cat, catfish, cheetah, cow, coyote, crab, crocodile, cuttlefish, deer, dog, dogfish, dolphin, eel, elephant, elk, ewe, fish, flying-fox, fowl, fox, frog, gazelle, giraffe, goat, gorilla, guanaco, halibut, hare, hedgehog, hippopotamus, horse, hyena, ichneumon, jackal, jaguar, kangaroo, leopard, lion, lioness, lizard, llama, lobster, lynx, marten, mongoose, monkey, mouse, octopus, opossum, otter, peccary, pig, porcupine, prawn, puma, python, rabbit, ram, reindeer, rhinoceros, various rodents, salmon, sardine, seal, sea-lion, sea-otter, sea-tortoise, serval, shark, shrew-mouse, skate, sloth, snake, squirrel, sword-fish, tapir, tiger, toad, tortoise, trout, turtle, wallaby, weasel, whale, wild-cat, wolf. Major insects are the ant, bee, beetle, butterfly, caterpillar, centipede, cicada, cricket, dragon-fly, earth-worm, firefly, fly, grasshopper, locust, mantis, moth, scorpion, spider, wasp, weevil and wood-worm (Waterbury, 1952, pp.4-5).

The following animals are also mentioned: the *t'ao-t'ieh*, dragon, rhinoceros, owl, hare, cicada, silkworm, turtle, fish, bird, phoenix, elephant, deer, the curling *kuei*, the frog and algae. Other common animals seen on An-Yang bronzes are oxen, water buffalo, sheep, tiger, bears, horses and boars (Chang, 1983, pp.56-57).

Despite strong minority views that animal designs developed out of geometric forms and therefore have no real intrinsic meanings, the ancient evidence tells otherwise. The animal motifs on the bronzes are linked, as far back as the Hsia Dynasty, to the ancient terms *wu* (animal offerings) and *chi* (ritual vessels). The *Tso Chuan* (606BC) records the reply of Wang-sun Man, emissary of King Ting of Chou, to King

Chuang of Chu's question about the *ting* tripods (Chang, 1983, pp.62-63):

> "Virtue not the tripods matter. Previously, when the Hsia dynasty was renowned for its virtue, the distant regions place into pictures their distinctive *wu* and the nine governors sent in metal of their provinces. The *ting* tripods were cast, those *wu* were represented on them. All *wu*s were represented and instructions were given for the preparations to be made in reference to them, so that the people might know how to distinguish between the benevolent and harmful spirits. So that the people while amidst the rivers, marshes, hills and forests did not meet injurious animals, and the hill-sprites, monstrous things and water-spirits did not meet them. Hence a harmony was maintained between the high and the low and all enjoyed the blessings of heaven."

Chang (1983, p.63) regards that the simple interpretation is that the animal designs or *wu* on the tripods assisted the ancient priests or shamans in the communications between heaven and earth. It is also obvious that to the ancient Chinese as far back as the Hsia Dynasty the animal designs are not meaningless but have magical significance, arising, as Chang (1983, p.74) notes, from their primary roles as the messengers of the spirit world.

Despite the high order of regard for some of these animals, the ancient Chinese have always regard Man as the most superior: The Four Intelligents (*Sze Ling*) are *Lung* alias the Dragon; *Feng Huang* the Phoenix; *Lin* the Unicorn; and *Gui* the Tortoise. They were not superior to man as man was considered the most intelligent creature. But the *Sze Lings* are believed to be endowed with special virtues for which they are respected and venerated (Wu, 1982, p.5).

The Chinese animal symbols seem many, complex and confusing. However, the purpose of this book is to show that the full significance of Chinese animal symbolisms could be systematically linked to the Chinese Ganzhi System.

THE GANZHI SYSTEM

Time is the essence of life and needs to be measured. Recording of events as in history needs measurement of time. The ancient Chinese measured time by the Ganzhi System, attributed to Danao, the adviser of the Yellow Emperor Huang-Ti (alias Gongsun or Hsien-Yang, 2677BC) (Wu, 1982). The system was probably older but Danao must have been instructed by the emperor to polish it up.

This Ganzhi System, full of cyclic signs, whose full secrets have been lost in ancient times, permeates several aspects of Chinese culture. While primarily the basis of the Chinese calendar and the popular Chinese Almanac, the *Tong-Shu* (Figure 2.1), its influence includes the geomantric art of *Feng-Shui* and its device the *Lo-Pan* (Figure 2.2), fortune telling and astrology. The Ganzhi System contains within it the secrets of the Chinese Eight Diagrams or Pakua (Figure 2.3).

The Ganzhi System has profound implications associated with Chinese animal symbolisms. The associations of time and direction with animals arose as animals are living moving creatures and hence suitable reflections of the interactions of time and direction.

Table 2.1

**Ganzhi System Twelve Terrestrial Branches
Estimation Of Time**

Animal		Month	Double	Direction	Western Zodiac	Planet
Tzu	Rat	mid-winter	11pm-1am	N	Sagittarius	Jupiter
Ch'ou	Ox	end-winter	1am-3am	N30E	Capricorn	Saturn
Yin	Tiger	early spring	3am-5am	N60E	Aquarius	Uranus
Mao	Hare	mid-spring	5am-7am	E	Pisces	Jupiter
Ch'en	Dragon	end-spring	7am-9am	S60E	Aries	Mars
Ssu	Snake	early-summer	9am-11am	S30E	Taurus	Venus
Wu	Horse	mid-summer	11am-1pm	S	Gemini	Mercury
Wei	Sheep	end-summer	1pm-3pm	S30W	Cancer	Moon
Shen	Monkey	early-autumn	3pm-5pm	S60W	Leo	Sun
Yu	Cock	mid-autumn	5pm-7pm	W	Virgo	Mercury
Hsu	Dog	end-autumn	7pm-9pm	N60W	Libra	Venus
Hai	Pig	early-winter	9pm-11pm	N30W	Scorpio	Mars

**Interpretations Of Ganzhi
twelve Terrestrial Branches Signs**

Animal				Gem
Tzu	Rat	yang	small child, beginning	Carbuncle
Ch'ou	Ox	yin	bound hand, binding, sustain	Onyx, white
Yin	Tiger	yang	greeetings, reverence	Sapphire
Mao	Hare	yin	open door, reception of Spring	Chrysolite
Ch'en	Dragon	yang	pregnant and timid	Amethyst
Ssu	Snake	yin	fully formed, seventh month of gestation	Mossagate
Wu	Horse	yang	struggle, opposition	Beryl
Wei	Sheep	yin	fully grown, mature	Emerald
Shen	Monkey	yang	expansion	Ruby
Yu	Cock	yin	vase for fermented drink	Jasper, pink
Hsu	Dog	yang	cutting, destruction, clearing the ground	Diamond
Hai	Pig	yin	propitious time for venturing	Topaz

Table 2.2

**Ganzhi System Ten Celestial Branches
Estimation Of Direction**

	Wood	**Fire**	**Earth**	**Metal**	**Water**
Direction	East	South	Centre	West	North
Colour	Blue-green	Red	Yellow	White	Black
Sacred Animal	Dragon Ox, Tortoise Dark Warrior	Phoenix	Dragon	Tiger	Snake
Class of animals	Scaly	Feathered	Naked	Hairy	Shell
Domestic animals	Sheep	Fowl	Ox	Dog	Pig
Orifice	Eyes	Ears	Mouth	Nose	Anus, vulva
Planet	Jupiter	Mars	Saturn	Venus	Mercury
Emperor	Fu-Hsi	Shen-Nung	Huang-Ti	Shao-hao	Chuan-Hsu
Qualities	Formidable	Burning	Cultivation	Changeable	Soaking
Weather	Wind	Heat	Sunshine	Cold	Rain
Organ	Liver	Heart	Spleen	Lungs	Kidney

Table 2.3

The Twenty-Eight Constellations Animals

No.	Hsiu	Object	Animal	Element	Auspiciousness
	East Azure Dragon Sector:				
1.	Chiao	Horn	Crocodile	Wood	auspicious
	Earth Dragon				
2.	K'ang	Neck	Sky Dragon	Metal	inauspicious
3.	Ti	Root	Badger	Earth	inauspicious
4.	Fang	Room	Hare	Sun	auspicious
5.	Hsin	Heart	Fox	Moon	auspicious
6.	Wei	Tail	Tiger	Fire	auspicious
7.	Chi	Basket	Leopard	Water	auspicious
	North Black Turtle Sector:				
8.	Nan tou	Ladle	Unicorn, Griffon	Wood	auspicious
9.	Niu	Buffalo	Buffalo	Metal	inauspcious
10.	Nu	Woman	Bat	Earth	inauspicious
11.	Hsu	Void	Rat	Sun	inauspicious
12.	Wei	Roof	Swallow	Moon	inauspicious
13.	Shih	House	Pig, Bear	Fire	auspicious
14.	Pi	Wall	Porcupine	Water	auspicious
	West White Tiger Sector				
15.	K'uei	Legs	Wolf	Wood	inauspicious
16.	Lou	Link	Dog	Metal	auspicious
17.	Wei	Stomach	Pheasant	Earth	auspicious
18.	Mao	Lights	Cock	Sun	inauspicious
19.	Pi	Thread	Crow, Raven	Moon	inauspicious
20.	Tsui	Turtle	Monkey	Fire	inauspicious
21.	Shen	3 associates (3 stars)	Gibbon	Water	auspicious
	Red Phoenix Sector				
22.	Ching	Well	Tapir	Wood	auspicious
23.	Kuei	Ghost	Goat, Sheep	Metal	inauspicious
24.	Liu	Willow	Buck	Earth	inauspicious
25.	Hsing	Star	Horse	Sun	inauspicious
26.	Chang	Fishing net, square	Stag	Moon	auspicious
27.	I	Wings	Snake	Fire	inauspicious
28.	Chen	Chariot	Earthworms	Water	auspicious

1 to 7 and their multiples correspond to the seven days of the week, starting with Thursday, and the seven planets Jupiter, Venus, Saturn, Sun, Moon, Mars and Mercury.

Figure 2.1: The Chinese Almanac, Tong-Shu – The Chinese Almanac provides advisory and divinatory guidelines on several aspects of the Chinese everyday life. Much of the advice is based on the Chinese Ganzhi System.

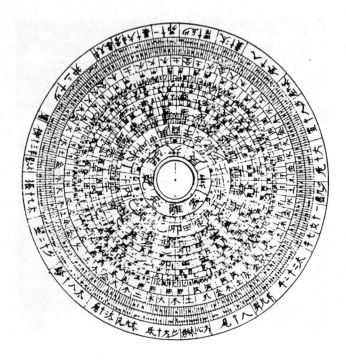

Figure 2.2: Lo-Pan, the plate used in the Chinese geomantric art of Feng Shui. The several rings of the Lo-Pan are actually elements of the Ganzhi system.

Figure 2.3 : The Pakua – Auspicious symbol of good fortune, happiness and longevity.

TEN CELESTIAL STEMS
AND TWELVE TERRESTRIAL BRANCHES

The Ganzhi System composes of twenty-two basic symbols grouped into two sets – ten belonging to *tiangan* (Ten Celestial Stems) and twelve belonging to *dizhi* (Twelve Terrestrial Branches) (Figure 2.4). The interaction of the twenty-two symbols of the Ten Celestial Stems and Twelve Terrestrial Branches control everything in the Universe. The two groups of this Ganzhi System are as follows:

A. Ten Celestial Stems (*Tiangan* or *Shih T'ien Kan*) also known as Ten Heavenly Stems or Denary series:

1. JIA (hard wood) trees
2. YI (soft wood) hewn timber
3. BING (sun fire) lightning
4. DING (kitchen fire) burning incense
5. WU (mountain earth) hills
6. JI (sand earth) earthenware
7. GENG (rough metal) metal ores
8. XIN (refined metal) kettles
9. REN (sea water) salt water
10. GUI (rain water) fresh water

These Ten Heavenly Stems reflect the plane of Heaven on the compass and not to Earth or Man although they do overlap on top of the planes of Earth and Man. They mark the positions of the constellations at the beginning of the New Year. The lucky stems are those of the 3, 4, 7 and 8 associated with the *Ken* and *Sun* trigrams, while unlucky stems are 1, 2, 9 and 10 associated with the *Ch'ien* and *Kun* trigrams which are strongly *Yang* and *Yin* with no admixture and therefore are unbalanced. 5 and 6 are central and neutral. 3 and 7 are *Yang* prosperity stems while 4 and 8 are *Yin* assistance stems. The Chinese word for "lucky" is a blend of prosperity and assistance.

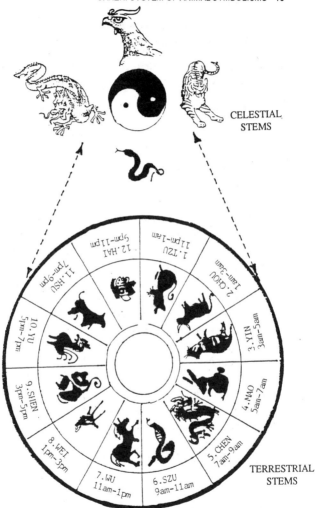

CELESTIAL STEMS

TERRESTRIAL STEMS

Figure 2.4: The Ganzhi System is an interaction between the forces of the Celestial Stems with their Twenty-eight Constellations and the Terrestrial Branches. This interaction is invoked in the Fang-Siang-Che Ceremony (Bear Dance).

Mythologically, the Ten Celestial Branches are represented by the Milky Way.

B. Twelve Terrestrial Branches (*Dizhi*) also known as Twelve Earthly Branches or Duodenary series:

1. ZI (rat)	7. WU (horse)
2. CHOU (ox)	8. WEI (sheep)
3. YIN (tiger)	9. SHEN (monkey)
4. MAO (horse)	10. YOU (cock)
5. CHEN (dragon)	11. XU (dog)
6. SI (serpent)	12. HAI (pig)

The Terrestrial Branches apply to factors on the Earth plane. The units of the *dizhi* system would be applied to the twelve units of times of the day (each unit being a double hour), the twelve months of the year and the twelve years corresponding to the famous twelve zodiacal animals. The twelve years compose one full Jupiter cycle. They also mark the twelve terrestrial directions and the location of the earth dragon *ch'i* forces.

Permuting the *tiangan* with the *dizhi* would produce a sixty-unit cycle, of Sexagenary Cycle, starting with *jiazi* (hard wood rat) and ending with *guihai* (rain water pig). Once the cycle is completed, it is repeated. This cycle is known as the *jiazi* cycle after the beginning of the sixty-unit which is "hard wood rat" or *jiazhi*.

ANIMALS OF THE GANZHI SYSTEM

The Ganzhi System is thus composed of two main sets of animal symbolisms as follow:

The *dizhi* Twelve Terrestrial Branches system is popularly known as the Twelve Zodiacal Animals (Figure 2.4, Table 2.1): rat, ox, tiger, hare, dragon, serpent, horse, sheep, monkey, cock, dog, and pig.

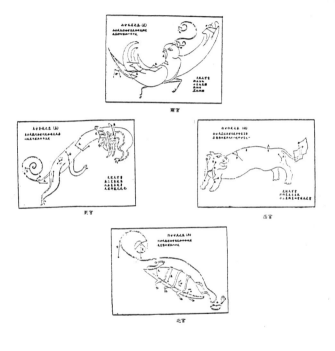

Figure 2.5: The Four Heraldic Animals of the Pakua. Top, South: Phoenix. Bottom, North: Tortoise-Snake. Left, East: Lung. Right, West: Tiger. These images are found in the Chinese Almanac, the Tong-Shu. Note the seven constellations for each animal, making a total of twenty-eight constellations for four of them.

On the other hand, the more complicated *tiangan* Celestial Stems system composes of the Five Elements, each with a hard or soft aspect. The *tiangan* Celestial Stems system is associated with the Four Heraldic or Supernatural Animals (Phoenix, *Lung*, Snake-Tortoise, Tiger – Figure 2.5) and also represent the Four Seasons; the fifth element, Earth at the centre, being represented by a second *Lung* (Table 2.2).

This *jiazi* cycle is a permutation of the Heraldic Animals of the *tiangan* system with the Zodiacal Animals of the *dizhi* system. Through the sixty years *jiazi* cycle, each zodiacal animal would be paired once with the *yin* or *yang* aspect of the Heraldic Animals.

The Ten Celestial Stems compose the oldest known cyclic signs. They feature on the oracles inscriptions (the then oldest Chinese texts of around 1400BC) linked to the calendar. The Twelve Terrestrial Branches were not fully defined until around the fifth century BC and were first used to designate the twelve hours of the day, then the twelve months and finally the twelve years of the Jupiter cycle. (de Kermadec and Poulsen, 1983, p.26). However, Ho (1975, p.240) notes that the legendary Hsia Emperors used the twenty-two letters of the Ganzhi System to help differentiate the sequence of their Emperors, suggesting that the Ganzhi System with both the Ten Celestial Stems and Twelve Terrestrial Branches could be far older; as old as the legendary Hsia Dynasty (2203-1766BC).

For practical purposes, the Ganzhi System with its two parallel systems of the *dizhi* Twelve Terrestrial Branches and the *tiangan* Ten Celestial Stems are the basis of Chinese astrology. The man would thus be influenced by one animal of the twelve zodiac animals and then also by one of the four-plus-one Heraldic Animals. The combination of the Twelve Terrestrial Branches with the Ten Celestial Stems comprehensively symbolizes the interactions of heavenly and earthly forces in the regulation of everything in the life of mankind. The Taoist priest would summon the heavenly or spirit powers through the Heraldic Animals but he also has to recognize the earthly forces represented by the Twelve Zodiacal Animals which especially reflect the characteristics of the person. The ancients know that the Ten Celestial Stems and Twelve Terrestrial Branches rule the entire destiny of Man.

ANIMALS OF THE
TWENTY-EIGHT CONSTELLATIONS

Outside the two main groups of the Ganzhi System, there are other refinements of the measurements of the Heaven and Earth. There is the 120 *fen-chin* which are the extension of the Ganzhi sixty units cycle.

An extension of the Ganzhi System which has intimate animal symbolism is the twenty-eight *hsiu* or smaller constellations of uneven sizes. These twenty-eight constellations cover a cycle of twenty-eight days. They are said to relate to the twenty-eight mansions of the moon of Western astrology and therefore show the position and movement of the moon through one lunar cycle. However, the synodic month, the time of one new moon to another, is about 29.5 days. The Twenty-Eight Constellations are more related to the sidereal month of 27.3 days, which is the time for the moon to return to the same position among the stars.

Although the Twenty-Eight Constellations have a twenty-eight days cycle, they are also related to the Four Seasons *tiangan* Celestial Stems system, as seven *hsiu* would be allocated to each of the four quadrants of Heaven. These *hsius* represent times when the geomancer would regard as most optimal to exert certain measures – something akin to the auspiciousness given to the new and full moon periods, believed to have influences on tidal movements and human sanity.

Each *hsiu* has its animal symbol and thus the Twenty-Eight Constellations give rise to twenty-eight animals (Table 2.3). Each of the four cardinal points Heraldic Animals would have seven animals. The animal symbolisms of the Twenty-Eight Constellations are an extension of the *tiangan* Ten Celestial Stems' Heraldic Animals symbolism.

It is quite clear that the Ganzhi System has at least three obvious basic groups of animal symbolisms:

1. The four-plus-one Heraldic Animals of the Ten Celestial Stems

2. The Twelve Zodiacal Animals

3. The Twenty-Eight Constellations Animals, which are an extension of the Ten Celestial Stems system.

However, some of the above animals have their alternative substitutes, which may include birds, insects and fish. Hence, by extension, the Ganzhi System could hold the true significance of the myriad of Chinese animal symbolisms.

Let us take a walk through the multi-coloured landscape of Chinese culture and have a good look at the animals arrayed therein. The throbs of the Chinese heart may be rediscovered among the legends and customs surrounding these animals throughout the ages. There are also connections to other cultures outside China. But behind all these so-called myths and legends of animals in China are the ramifications of ancient Chinese thoughts regarding the sacredness of life.

THE FOUR HERALDIC ANIMALS

A very powerful cyclic layer of significance, and the most auspicious of the Ganzhi System, is that the cardinal points of North, West, South, East, linked to the *tiangan* Ten Celestial Stems, are associated with the Chinese Four Heraldic Animals: the Snake, Tiger, Phoenix and *Lung* (Figure 3.1). These Four Heraldic Animals with strong relationships to the Five Elements occupy important positions in several aspects and rituals of the ancient Chinese culture.

The ancient Chinese has considered the *Lung* as the chief of the Four Spiritual Animals. The Four Spiritual Animals are: (Plopper, 1935, p.47)

1. The *Ling* or Unicorn
2. The Phoenix
3. The Tortoise
4. The Dragon.

The Unicorn, the Phoenix, the Tortoise, and the Dragon are the four spiritual creatures. (Plopper, 1935, p.113).

The arrangements of the Four Supernatural Animals and the Four Spiritual Animals are not essentially different. This is because the Snake is often replaced by the Tortoise (Black Warrior). The hairy animal representing the West could be the Tiger, the Bear or the Unicorn (Hsu and Ward, 1984, p.467).

The ancient Chinese truly regard Man as superior to these powerful Heraldic Animals: The Four Intelligents (*Sze Ling*) are *Lung* alias the Dragon; *Feng Huang* the Phoenix; *Lin* the Unicorn; and *Gui* the Tortoise. They were not superior to man as man is considered the most intelligent creature. But these

Sze Lings are believed endowed with special virtues for which they are respected and venerated (Wu, 1982, p.5).

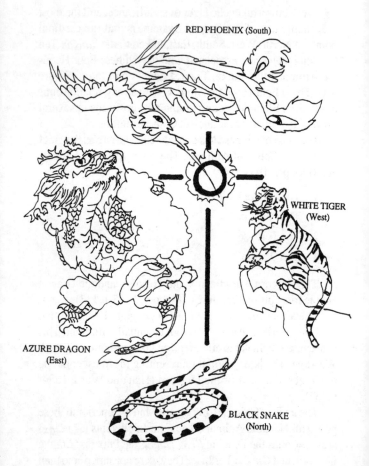

RED PHOENIX (South)

WHITE TIGER
(West)

AZURE DRAGON
(East)

BLACK SNAKE
(North)

Figure 3.1: The Chinese Four Symbolic Animals

The Ten Celestial Stems compose of the dark and light aspects of the Five Elements – fire, wood, water, metal, earth, and these are symbolized by the Four Heraldic Animals: In *The Five Elements*, according to the Former Heaven Sequence, the five elements of wood, fire, earth, metal, water correspond respectively to east, south, centre, west and north. They are also connected respectively to the five animals of azure dragon, red phoenix, yellow dragon, white tiger and black snake-tortoise and the five emperors Fu-Hsi, Shen-Nung, Huang-ti, Shao-hao and Chuan-hsu (Skinner, 1982, Table 5, pp.58-59).

The above association of the Pakua aspect of the Ganzhi System with the Five Emperor Gods is the basis of many powerful charms. These Four Heraldic Animals are the source of power summoned during Taoist magic or spiritual rituals.

The Five Elements and their associated Four Heraldic Animals represent an ancient knowledge of how heavenly forces could be manipulated to affect earthly destinies. The central rituals of Taoist magic, following the sequences of the *Lo-Shu*, consist in the ability to call up these forces of these Spirit-Generals and indicate that these Pakua Five Elements-Four Heraldic Animals are the essence of supernatural powers. That is why the Chinese call them the Four Supernatural Animals.

The basic four Heraldic Animals of Azure Dragon, Red Phoenix, White Tiger and Black Snake-Tortoise are also seen in Chinese astrology: Seven stellar 'mansions' were located to each of the four quadrants of heaven which are linked with four animals. The Azure Dragon governing the eastern quarter, the Vermilion Bird (Chinese Phoenix) the southern, the White Tiger the western and the Black Warrior (Tortoise) the northern. The morning sun is the east and Spring; at noon it is south or Summer. The west corresponds to Autumn and the north to Winter. The Great Bear has a prominent position in the heavens as the aerial throne of the Taoist Supreme God, Shang Ti, to whom other star-gods circulate in homage. The Northern Dipper (Shou Hsing), a group of stars in Ursa Major with the Southern Dipper (Lu Hsing) in the southern heavens represents the Gods of Longevity and Wealth. The Queen of Heaven or Mother of the Measure or Buddhist Goddess Maritchi who dwells among the stars of the Dipper or Great Bear is also worshipped (William, 1931, pp.336-340).

The Four Heraldic Animals also correspond respectively to the Four Major Seasons of Winter, Summer, Autumn and Spring. This symbolism is shown in Table 2.2. The ending period of each season is a transient period. These four transient times in the year are attributed to the fifth Heraldic Animal at the Centre and to the Yellow or Golden *Lung*.

As Table 2.2 indicates, the alternate animals for the Phoenix, Tiger and Snake are respectively the Fowl, Dog and Pig. The *Lung* has two alternate animals; the Sheep for the Azure *Lung* and the Ox for the Golden *Lung*.

FOUR HERALDIC ANIMALS
ARE SYMBOLS OF FOUR MIGHTY ANGELS

The Four Heraldic Animals are symbols of four great spirit generals. Chinese Taoism regards the Four Heraldic Animals as the Four Heavenly Kings (or Buddhist *Chinkangs*) (Williams, 1931) who control the four spheres of Heaven (Figure 3.2):

1. Guardian of the East. Land Bearer. White face, ferocious appearance, copper beard, carries a jade ring, a spear, magic sword.

2. Guardian of the West. Far-Gazer. Blue-face, carries four-stringed guitar.

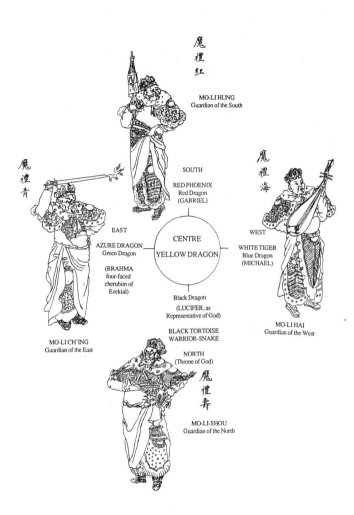

Figure 3.2: The Four Buddhist Chinkangs, also known as Four Taoist Heavenly Kings.

3. Guardian of the South. Lord of Growth. Red face, holds an umbrella.

4. Guardian of the North. Well-famed. Black face, has two whips, bag, and snake.

These Four Beings are commonly known in other forms in the Chinese culture:

In the worship of the Nine Emperor Gods, the East, West, South, North and Centre are guarded by the Green, White, Red, Black and Yellow Dragons or Generals (Cheu, 1988).

Both English and Chinese specialists disagree in minor details in connecting the Buddhist *Chinkang* with the Taoist Heavenly Kings (Plopper, 1935, p.175). The following comparison is probably correct. They are:

1. To Wen or Mo Li Shou, who watches over the north and winter. He is black (the Black Warrior) and holds a snake in his hands.

2. Tseng Ch'ang or Mo Li Hung, who watches over the south, and summer. He is red and carries an umbrella.

3. Ch'i Kuo or Mo Li Hai, who watches over the east and spring. He is blue and carries a guitar in his hands.

4. Kuang Mu or Mo Li Ch'ing, who watches over the west and autumn. He is white and carries a sword

These four spirit animal-generals are very old entities in Chinese culture. Among the Chinese deities from very ancient times, only the imageless Shang-Ti the Supreme God and the above four non-human *Chinkangs* were not from human origins. These four spirit beings have parallels in other cultures.

THE FOUR BIBLICAL ANGELIC SPHERES

An ill-understood feature is that the Christian Bible frequently refers to these same four groups of angels of the Four *Chinkangs* of the Eight Diagrams-Pakua. Let us now examine where the Bible mentions the four groups of angels:

Saying to the sixth angel which had the trumpet, "Loosen the four angels which are bound at the great river Euphrates". And the four angels were loosen which were prepared for an hour and a day and a month and a year, to slay a third of the men ... (Revelation 9:14-15)

And round about the throne were four and twenty seats and upon the seats I saw four and twenty elders sitting clothed in white garments ... and round about the throne were four beasts full of eyes in front and behind (Revelation 4:4-6).

And before the throne ... were four beasts full of eyes in front and behind. And the first beast was like a lion and the second beast like a calf, and the third beast had a face like a man's, and the fourth beast was like a flying eagle. And the four beasts had each of them six wings round about and underneath and they were full of eyes within and they rest not day and night saying: " Holy, holy, holy, Lord God Almighty which was, and is, and is to come." (Revelation 4:6-8)

And one of the four beasts gave unto the seven angels seven golden vials full of the wrath of God who liveth forever and ever. (Revelation 15:7)

Now the cherubims stood on the right side of the house when the man went in and the cloud filled the inner court ... And when I looked behold the four wheels by the cherubims, one wheel by one cherub

and another wheel by another cherub: and the appearance of the wheels was as the colour of a beryl
stone ... And every one had four faces: the first face
was the face of a cherub, and the second face was the
face of a man, and the third the face of a lion and the
fourth the face of an eagle ... And the cherubims ...
stood at the door of the east gate of the Lord's house ...
(Ezekiel 10:3,9,14,19 – verse 9 suggests there were
four cherubims)

So, winged angelic creatures resembling the lion, the calf
and the eagle exist as described in the Bible. Not to mention
the snake which is the symbol of Satan. The Bible clearly has
these same spirit heraldic animals as the Chinese culture!

The *Shan Hai Ching* (from early first millennium BC) associates the Double *Lungs* with carrying agents bringing mes-
sages back and forth between heaven and earth (Chang, 1983,
p.65). Oracle bones inscriptions also show that Shang-Ti the
Supreme God was believed to have been served by many officials including the messenger Phoenix (Chang, 1983, p.68).
The *Lung* and the Phoenix are therefore regarded as the messengers of God. So, they are really the same as angels of the
Bible – for the word "angel" means messenger of God.

Under each of these four main angels there is a hierarchy
of lower angels. According to the traditions of the Dato of the
island of Pulau Tikus in Penang, Malaysia, the Dato spirit is
only one of the seven lieutenants. These lieutenants are under
a General Spirit who rules over the Malayan Main Range that
stretches from southern Thailand. Chances are this General
Spirit is under the East Angel of the Lord. It is important to
note these locational hierarchies, for the spirits have their territories and may not intervene into other territories. This is a
feature often noticed in demon exorcism. That the demons
have their territories and may not cross certain borders; this

fact could be used to exorcise a person by getting him to move into another place!

The hierarchy of angels under each major angel numbers seven. This is actually the *hsius* of the Twenty-Eight Constellations.

KABALIC ASSOCIATIONS OF
FOUR DIRECTIONS WITH ANGELIC BEASTS

Also striking are the parallels of the Chinese Four Heraldic Animals in the Jewish Kabala system. In its Tenth Key of the Tarot (Figure 3.3) the Jewish Kabala associates four animals with the cardinal points (Levi, 1825-1875):

1. Top, South Woman headed Sphinx. Woman front, lion forebody and claws, eagle wings and ox backbody and tail. (Chinese parallel = Phoenix)

2. Left, East Kerub – Bull-Horned Bearded Man headed Sphinx. Bull-Horned Bearded Man front, backbody-tail of fish. (Chinese parallel = *Lung*)

3. Bottom, North Typhon. The double Serpents. (Chinese parallel = Snake)

4. Right, West Dog-headed Sphinx. Dog head, man's body. (Chinese parallel – Tiger. *Feng-Shui* domestic equivalent of Tiger is Dog)

The North-South alignment of the Chinese Snake-Phoenix is the Hebrew Double-Snake-Winged Sphinx. The Hebrew has the Dog where the Chinese has the Tiger. The Hebrew figure opposite the Dog is a bull-horned bearded man with a fish-tail lower body. Careful comparison would show this Hebrew man-fish is really the same as the Chinese *Lung*!

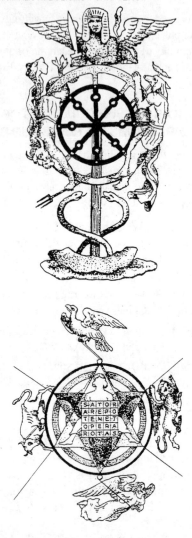

Figure 3.3: Kabalic arrangements of four animals.
Top: Tenth Key of Tarot. Bottom: William Poster's version.

Also, in the Chinese system, the domestic animal which is the equivalent of the Tiger is actually the Dog! Then the parallelism between the Chinese and Hebrew Four Animals is completely similar. This position of the Tiger-Dog is also substituted with a Unicorn (the Chinese *Ki-lin*) by both Chinese and Hebrew, while the Hebrew may replace the Dog with the Lion. The Snake could be replaced in the Chinese system by the Tortoise or Dark Warrior. In the Hebrew Kabalic system, the Snake is sometimes replaced by a winged man cherubim.

CONFUSION BETWEEN CHINESE LUNG AND SNAKE

In the Chinese Four Heraldic Animals, the *Lung* alias the Dragon in the East is a different animal from the Snake in the North. Despite these differences some people have persistently confused the Chinese *Lung* with the Serpent of the Bible.

The connection between the Chinese Black Snake of the North with the Jewish Kabalic Typhon-double Snakes is quite clear.

The Chinese *Lung* is the Kabalic Kerub a bull-horned bearded man with limbed forefront and a fish backbody and tail. This bull-headed sphinx is featured in Assyrian, Egyptian and Indian hieroglyphs (Levi, 1835, p.137) and also is the angel placed to prevent Adam and Eve from re-entering the Garden of Eden to partake of the Tree of Life. The Bible indicates that this gate of the Garden was at the east – the Chinese *Lung* is at the east.

In the Kabala system this Kerub, a bearded horned fish-tailed being, is a different angelic creature from the limbless Typhon Snakes. It should be obvious too that the Chinese *Lung* which is the bearded horned fish-tailed being, should not be associated with the Biblical or Kabalic Dragon-Snake.

THE SPECIAL CLASS OF
CHERUBIMS KNOWN AS SERAPHIM

A host of angelic animals compose those marvellous creatures known as cherubs or cherubims known to Biblical and
Middle East lores. These cherubs or cherubims have many
forms (Peloubet, 1947):

> The Cherub is a symbolic figure, a composite crea-
> ture-form which is paralleled in religious insignia of
> Assyria, Persia and Egypt, e.g. the sphinx, the winged
> bulls and lions of Nineveh. Paradise is guarded by a
> cherub (Genesis 3:24). Cherubim figures were placed·
> on the mercy seat of the ark (Exodus 25:18). The ark
> in Solomon's temple was overshadowed by the
> canopy of their contiguously extended wings of a
> colossal pair (1 Kings 6:27) Surprisingly, with precise
> directions as to their position, attitude and material,
> nothing, save they were winged, is said about their
> shape. It is likely that the word "cherub" meant not
> only the composite creature=form, of which the man,
> lion, ox and eagle were the elements, but, further,
> some peculiar and mystical form. (Ezekiel 1:6)

Each of these cherubims could be an individual angelic
animal or could be a composite beast. Besides the above, the
Bible also referred to those unique creatures, known in the
Jewish Kabala system as "seraphim":

> Above it stood the *seraphim* [8314]: each has six
> wings; with twain he covered his face and with twain
> he covered his feet and with twain he did fly. And one
> cried unto another and said, Holy, holy, holy is the
> Lord of hosts; the whole earth is full of his glory ...
> (Isaiah 6:2-3)

Then flew one of the *seraphim* [8314] unto me, having a live coal in his hand which he had taken with the tongs from the altar ... (Isaiah 6:6)

The *seraphim* are a special class of cherubims. While the *seraphim* may embrace a range of angelic animals, the Isaiah's *seraphim* has "hands" to enable it to handle a tong to collect the coal. Note too that the Isaiah's *seraphim* have some similarities (though may or may not be the same) as the four beasts in Revelation chapter 4 in:

> having six wings
> having limbs
> praising God "Holy, holy, holy" all the time.

The *seraphim* are said to be "an order of celestial beings ... act as the medium of communication between heaven and earth" (Peloubet, 1947, seraphim). The *seraphim* are therefore of the world of God's angelic beasts and they are a special class of cherubs or cherubims. The *seraphim* may denote holy angelic beasts of God.

The word "seraphim" is from the Hebrew *saraph* which is from another *saraph* (coded 8314) which is in turn is from another *saraph* (coded 8313 – primary root meaning being to "set on fire", to burn or kindle). Hence, *saraph* came to denote the fiery nature of a creature – the angelic *seraphim* of Isaiah 6:2-3, 6 and also the fiery serpent [8314] of Numbers 21:8 which Moses placed on a pole to counter the bites of serpents [5175]:

And the Lord sent fiery [8314] serpents [5175] among the people and they bit the people and much people died ... And the Lord said unto Moses, Make thee a fiery [8314] serpent [also 8314] and set it upon a pole and it shall come to pass that every one that is bitten when he looketh upon it he lived. And Moses

made a serpent [5175] of brass and put it on a pole and
it came to pass that if a serpent [5175] had bitten any
man when he beheld the serpent [5175] of brass he
lived ... (Numbers 21:6-9)

There appears some associations between the *nachash*
serpent and the *saraph* seraphim. But this strange creature the
Isaiah's *seraphim* is a fiery creature and possesses wings and
"hands". It seems associated with a serpentine body form like
the limbless serpent but is different in that the Isaiah's
seraphim has wings and hands.

Therefore, the Isaiah's *seraphim* is a sort of serpentine
animal with wings and hands like the Chinese *Lung*!

The Chinese *Lung* alias the 'Dragon' is one of the holy
seraphim of God mentioned in the Holy Scriptures! It is different from the *nachash* serpent which is the symbol of Satan.
The *nachash* serpent of the Bible is an animal associated with
evil – and the Chinese while associating its Chinese *Lung*
alias 'Dragon' with good auspicious things, do indeed associate similarly the Snake with evil.

The truth is that the Biblical Dragon-Serpent is one of the
cherubims while the Chinese *Lung* is another different type of
cherubim! While the Biblical Dragon-Serpent is a fallen
angel (namely Satan), the Chinese *Lung* remains a faithful
cherubim of God.

The Bible calls the Serpent evil, the Chinese do the same
thing. The Bible call the *seraphim* holy of God – the Chinese
do the same thing for its *Lung* alias 'dragon'. All these times,
the Chinese are correct to maintain their *Lung* alias 'Dragon'
as the symbol of the Godly. Repeat: The Chinese *Lung* is the
holy *seraphim* of God!

Another thing is this: the Jewish Kabalic system regards
seraphim as the highest of the angels. There are many levels
of angels. There are also many levels of archangels, and the
highest are the *seraphim*. The Chinese *Lung*, with the rest of

the Four Heraldic Animals, are among the highest angelic beings!

The Chinese Four Supernatural Animals are representations of the Four Groups of the highest Angels of God. These beings are not just mighty angels but the highest angels. It is not a wonder that the ancient Chinese called them the Four Heavenly Kings or Four *Chinkangs* who surrounded the throne of Shang-Ti the Supreme God.

A THOUGHT ABOUT THE HERALDIC ANIMALS

The Kabalic arrangements of four animals in the Middle East ancient cultures are thus strikingly similar to the Chinese Pakua arrangement of the Four Heraldic Animals. It is very evident that the Pakua symbol of the Four Heraldic Animals has universal existence and parallel similar significance in many cultures, including those of ancient China and Middle East.

They could not have arisen independently but must have originated from common sources. There can only be a diffusion of this Pakua Four Animals symbol into the different cultures.

The comparison between the Chinese and Middles East angelic animals also suggests a fundamental basis of the animal symbolism: much of the animal symbolism reflects the images of spirits which include the highest of the angels like cherubims and seraphim. Which is why, ever since the earliest beginnings of mankind, the ancient records show these animal images playing many roles in ancient magic and worship rituals and sacrifices.

4

THE COLOURFUL PHOENIX

Linked with Falcon, Eagle, Pheasant, Peacock, Stork, Heron, Egret, also with "Fire-Star" Antares in the southern constellation of Scorpio.

One of the delightful Chinese animals is the elegant colourful bird, known as Phoenix, or *Feng Huang*, the Heraldic Animal of the South (Figure 4.1). The Phoenix is a common auspicious emblem found in Chinese art and crafts. There is a Chinese saying which goes:

"Good fortune of the Dragon and Phoenix"

The Phoenix is a fabulously colourful bird of mystical and wondrous nature and is one of the four supernatural creatures. It is also known as the Vermilion or Red Bird in the art of Chinese *Feng-Shui*, being the creature of the South. The other three animals are the Azure Dragon in the East, the Black Tortoise or Dark Warrior (or Snake) to the North and the White Tiger to the West. The Phoenix is the emperor among the birds just as the Unicorn is king of the four-legged beasts (Williams, p.286). The Phoenix is also one of the Four Intelligent Animals.

DESCRIPTION

It has the head of a pheasant, the crown of a mandarin duck, the beak of a swallow, the back of a tortoise and the tail of a fish. Often it is a composite of the peacock and the pheasant with the addition of many colours (Dennys, p.112; Williams, p.286). The tail has twelve feathers. Each of the five colours of the bird's plumage is typical of each of its cardinal virtues.

鳳凰

Figure 4.1: The Auspicious Phoenix or Feng Huang.
Symbol of the sun and warmth shining in from the South. Appears
only in reigns of virtuous rulers. The enemy of the evil snake. Note
that the character Feng Huang illustrates a bird trapped under a
cage. The old oracle bone character for Feng Huang was a free
bird. The once free Phoenix is no longer free but would one day be
free again.

The female phoenix is called *Huang* and this name combined with the male *Feng* forms the compound word *Feng Huang* (Figure 4.2). It is five cubits tall (Williams, p.286). A cubit is an ancient measure of length, approximately equal to the length of a forearm. Viewed from the front it looks like a wild swan and from the rear, like a unicorn. It has a serpent's neck, a fish's tail, a dragon's scales, a tiger's back, a swallow's jowl and throat and a rooster's beak (Wu, p.6).

The Phoenix will feast in the Vermilion Hills until peace prevails in the outer world. When the Phoenix comes out on one of its rare journeys, it would be accompanied by a train of other birds. The Chinese may have a painting of the Phoenix surrounded by one hundred different birds. It feeds only on bamboo seeds and drinks from sweet springs. Its voice is like a wondrous song (Williams, p.286).

It alights only on the *Wu-T'ung* tree and never threads on living herbs. The *Wu-T'ung* tree, or *dryanda (Sterculia plantiflora)*, is ornamental, with bell flowers and large leaves, and grows to a great height swiftly. The leaves open early and fall in autumn. The seeds are used in moon-cakes during the Eighth Moon of the Mid-Autumn Festival. The Phoenix is a benevolent solitary bird which, like the Unicorn, never hurt other creatures (Williams, p.286), except the venomous Serpent.

The Phoenix lives for five hundred years, flies to Heliopolis to be burnt to ashes on the altar. A young Phoenix rises on the third day and flies away to live another five hundred years (Whittick, 1960, p.237). The bird is thus the product of the sun and fire. The Phoenix may be depicted gazing at the ball of the sun (Williams, p.286); a trait said to be true also of the Falcon.

Its rarity, as compared to the more "common" *Lung*, is said to be due to its eggs being the food of fairies (Burkhardt, 1982, p.188).

AUSPICIOUS MEANINGS OF THE PHOENIX

The Chinese Phoenix symbolizes the sun and warmth for summer and harvest (Williams, p.286).

In ancient times this bird appeared during the reigns of virtuous rulers and would grace such governments as their emblem (Dennys, 1968, p.112). The Phoenix was said to appear first in the courts of Huang-Ti, the Yellow Emperor when the sovereign observed the ceremonial fasts. Two Phoenixes were in Yao's palace about 2350BC. It also came to add splendour to the musical ceremonies of the great Emperor Shun (Dennys, 1968, p.112; Williams, 1931, p.288). Legend has it that it came when Confucius was born (Williams, 1931, p.286). The Phoenix became an object of worship during the Han Dynasty (Burkhardt, 1982, p.188). Claims of the visits of Phoenixes were often made to proclaim a successful reign or justify a succession including the founding of a new dynasty, for example, that of the Ming Dynasty. So, along this vein we have several sayings about the Phoenix:

- Phoenixes also act as harbinger of the births of great men.
- The Phoenix will land only when there is something precious around.
- The Phoenix brings prosperity.
- When it appears the world will enjoy great peace and ease.
- The Taoist symbol is that "Nine-Phoenix symbol for the destruction of filth" (Lagerway, 1967, p.73).

The Phoenix, as an emblem of beauty, was also employed by female members of the royal family as a beautiful headdress ornament, like the vulture headdress of Egyptian women.

Figure 4.2: The Phoenix-Lung Symbol on the invitation card to a wedding dinner

Even as *Lung* is the Imperial symbol of the Emperor, the Phoenix is the Imperial symbol of the Empress. The pairing of *Lung* with Phoenix is a popular symbol, often indispensable as decorative motifs during marriages (Figure 4.2).

Early Christians adopted it on catacombs, mosaics and manuscripts as the symbol of resurrection and immortality (Whittick, 1960, p.237). In ancient Egypt, it was a symbol of the sun and the Phoenix was similar to the Stork, Heron or Egret. It also became the symbol of imperial apotheosis. The Arabian Phoenix is a kind of Eagle (Williams, 1931, p.286). The sphinx was a common Egyptian symbol of power. The earliest Egyptian sphinx has a lion's body and a bearded man's head, the latter being the head of the reigning monarch. There were three main types of sphinxes, each with a lion's resting body (Whittick, 1960, pp.263-265):

1. Androsphinx, with a man's head

2. Hieracosphinx, with a falcon's head

3. Criosphinx, with a ram's head

The Egyptian Hieracosphinx is a version of the Phoenix, suggesting its similarity to the Falcon. The Assyrians had similar sphinxes as the Egyptians except that usually the lion would be walking and wings were added. Another version of the Phoenix is the griffin, griffon or gryphon which has the body of a lion but the head and wings of the eagle. It function is to guard treasures and is the symbol of watchfulness. There are many representations of the griffin in ancient Assyria and Greece (Whittick, 1960, pp.194, 263-265).

Some have tried to differentiate the Chinese Phoenix from the western Phoenix (Burkhardt, 1982, p.187). The western Phoenix is said to be a bird of prey as evidenced by its curved beak. But the Chinese Phoenix is gallinaceous with a beak and head more alike to the Pheasant or the Peacock.

AUSPICIOUS LEGENDS ABOUT PHOENIX

The Purifying Power Of The Phoenix

In the Hebrew Kabalic philosophy the Phoenix is the symbol of the Holy Spirit, indicating its supreme status as a symbol of God's power. One significance of the Phoenix is its role as the enemy of evil.

The Chinese is not ignorant of this power of the Phoenix. In Taoist mysticism, the high priest would write onto a yellow slip of paper: "Nine-Phoenix symbol for the destruction of filth" (Lagerway, 1967, p.73). He would light the paper and allow it to burn almost to his fingers and then blows it into the air. The symbol is regarded in Taoism as the purifying role of fire – this is paralleled by western symbolism of the Phoenix as the bird rising, resurrected, from the flames.

The Phoenix is the Heraldic Animal of the South whose Taoist number is nine, hence the term "Nine-Phoenix". It appears that the significance of the Phoenix status was also appropriated by the nine-*Lungs* symbol. The number "Nine" is rightfully the number of the Phoenixes and not the *Lung*. That is, the nine-*Lungs* symbol is the secret Taoist knowledge that nine *Lungs* combined are still inferior to the Phoenix. This should not be surprising, since the *Lung* is the symbol of the priest-king Chinese emperor and therefore the symbol of nature's high power, while the Phoenix is really the symbol of God's supreme power.

The Phoenix used to be "seen" during the reigns of the legendary emperors and it was at the Emperors Huang-Ti and Shun times were the last when they were more frequently seen. But now the Phoenix was not available to mankind. Its power could only be symbolized vaguely by nine-*Lungs*. The Taoist knows so and the Chinese preserves this indication of the unavailability of the Phoenix in its character for *Feng Huang* as in Figure 4.1. The character really symbolizes the bird hidden under a shell, denoting its existence but not free.

The character is an ancient prophecy that such a power exists and being not yet available would one day be available.

The Scorpio Link

The purifying power of the Chinese Phoenix is known in western Kabalic philosophy. An ancient hint about the power of the Phoenix against evil is found in the astrological significance of the southern constellation of Scorpio, which has a good "Eagle" form in contrast against a bad "Scorpion" form.

The Chinese Phoenix, as the Heraldic Animal of the South, is associated with planet Mars. The southern constellation of the Hebrew is Scorpio which is chiefly marked by the brightest star, the huge red star Antares well known in Chinese astronomy as the "Fire-Star" (Needham, 1959). Scorpio is also associated with Mars. In its "Eagle" form, the western Scorpio is thus analogous to the Chinese Phoenix.

The Scorpio in Hebrew astrology has two aspects, one the generous, refined, reliable and astute being of the good "Eagle" Scorpio, while the bad "Snake" Scorpio will be destructive, unreliable, deceitful, irascible, calumniators and prevaricators (Joel, 1977, p.71). In western astrology the Scorpio has its scorpion form or its eagle form (Lutin, 1988). Hence, the Scorpio is either an Eagle or a Snake-Scorpion depending on the circumstances.

The western astrology recognizes the southern constellation of Scorpio as either the biting Scorpion dying of its own poison in its struggle for survival, or the noble Eagle the healer and magician who battles the forces of evil and darkness and triumph (Lutin, 1988, p.11). The unafraid Eagle is the embodiment of truth and lives to heal the wounds of his fellow beings. Fear and evil flees from the noble Eagle which wings into heaven in joyous celebration of victory.

*Figure 4.3: The "Three Realms" Phoenix-Lung deities (left) as
compared to Kabalic Hermes Bird (right)*

The bird is at the top level in both arrangements.
Immediately below are two Dragon-Lungs along the second level
of both arrangements. In the Chinese arrangement, the two Lungs
are associated with five deities. At the lowest and third levels are
eight persons. Both the Chinese and Kabalic have strikingly
similiar concepts of the "Three Realms"!

Scorpio is thus the representation of conflict. It has three decans all symbolizing conflicts (Seiss, 1972, p.18):

1. The Serpent with which Ophiuchus struggled
2. Ophiuchus, struggling with the Serpent and being stung by the Scorpion also crushing the Scorpion
3. Hercules holding the three-headed snake or dog of hell.

The significance of Scorpio is that the conflicts represented by the three decans of Scorpio are the tasks of Ophiuchus and Hercules in preventing the seizure by the Serpent of the Crown (in nearby Libra) which is located just above the Serpent's mouth.

The Taoist "Nine-Phoenix" symbol for the destruction of filth (Lagerway, 1967, p.73) is part of the esoteric Taoist Thunder Magic which is used against the malevolent Mao Shan Serpent Black Magic. That is, the Chinese "Nine-Phoenix" has the same significance as the Kabalic Scorpio in that they represent the fight of the Phoenix against the Serpent.

The Christian writers Seiss (1972) and Flemings (1981) picture Scorpio as representing the suffering Christ in his mortal struggles against the forces of evil. We know that the Christians represent Christ as risen from the death in victory over Satan the Serpent; alike to the Phoenix-like resurrection from the purifying fire!

The southern Chinese Phoenix or Scorpio is therefore the symbol of the age-old work of God's supreme power in overcoming barriers to purify. There is a secret cost to God as evident by the suffering this symbol represents. The goal is the eternal Crown – but this crown is forbidden to the evil and wicked, implying only the good and the courageous could ever hope to achieve it. The Devil the Serpent evidently sought it but failed, being blocked by God.

Phoenix is the symbol of the supreme mystic forbidden art required to reach the crown.

The supreme art requires the supreme power of the Holy Spirit of God which is represented by the Eagle Scorpio-Phoenix Bird. A sacrificial attitude is required to master this supreme art.

THE MARRIAGE SYMBOL OF DRAGON-PHOENIX

There are certain pairs of animals which form auspicious symbols in the Chinese culture, like two Dragons with the dragon pearl between them or two lions playing with a ball. Most significant of all is the pairing of the *Lung* and the Phoenix with the "pearl" between them often seen in wedding cards (Figure 4.2).

What is the real significance of the Phoenix-*Lung* symbol and its saying "Good fortune of the *Lung*-Phoenix"?

Why is it so widely used in wedding ceremonies? The Dragon is supposed to be the symbol of the male force while the Phoenix that of the female, representing respectively the bridegroom and the bride. However, there are certain reason(s) why this symbol is associated with the marriage ceremony!

The "paired Phoenix-*Lung*" symbol is also found in the Hebrew Kabalic philosophy. The Phoenix is known as the Hermes Bird in the Hebrew Kabalic philosophy where the Hermes Bird is also paired with the dragon (Shumaker, 1972, p.195). This is illustrated in Figure 4.3, an obvious parallel to the Chinese symbolical pairing of the Phoenix-*Lung*.

A double headed Dragon is shown, the heads facing away from each other. The mouth of one head opens to a gold sun and the other mouth to a silver moon and this has obvious parallels to the Chinese "dragon pearl" which could be a moon or sun. The dragon body is a fish rear body and the animal seems to be a mer-animal, which again has parallels to the Chinese *Lung*, which is primarily a water creature. Above the doubled headed Dragon is shown the Hermes Bird coming down through the clouds. This Hermes Bird is regarded as the symbol of the Holy Spirit descending from the Father hidden by the clouds.

In this pairing of the two fabulous creatures, the Phoenix and the *Lung*, ten qualities are signified:

Left:	Cunning or Knowledge	**Right:**	Grace
	Experience		Nature
	Practice		Reason
	Prudence		Speculative Faculty
	Patience		Holy Living

While the simpler form of the pair is the *Lung*-Phoenix on the wedding cards (Figure 4.3), the Chinese also has a more complicated arrangement as in Figure 4.5, representing the Three Realms (Huang, 1986, p.71). This Chinese version, from the Ching dynasty, is like the Hermes Bird version.

The Three Realms are Heaven, Earth and Man. Right at the top is the single god riding a Phoenix representing Heaven. Note the two *Lung*s below the Phoenix – the two *Lung*s hang over five persons symbolizing the Five Emperors, representing Earth. Then below these Five Emperors are eight persons for Man – these eight persons also correspond to the eight persons besides the two-headed Dragon of the Hermes Bird. The similarities between the Chinese paired *Lung*-Phoenix and the Hebrew Hermes Bird-two headed Dragon are striking.

THE MARRIAGE FEAST OF GOD

The Scorpio-symbolized final outcome of the battles between the forces of good and evil is not unknown to the Christian mystics. The Bible shows this in a passage from the book of Revelation:

Let us be glad and rejoice, and give honour to Him
for the Marriage of the Lamb is come and His wife
hath made herself ready ... Blessed are they which are
called unto the marriage supper of the Lamb ... And I
saw an angel standing in the sun; and he cried out with
a loud voice, saying to all the Fowls that fly in the
midst of heaven. Come and gather yourselves
together unto the supper of the great God; that ye may
eat the flesh of kings, and the flesh of captains, and the
flesh of mighty men and the flesh of horses, and of
them that sit on them, and the flesh of all men, both
free and bond, both small and great. (Revelation 19:7-
9, 17-18)

The Bible connects the symbol of "Fowls eating up the
powers of evil" as the "Marriage of the Lamb"! Note who
fights the battle. The battle is seen as the fight of God over the
evil enemies of His people:

"As birds flying so will the Lord of hosts defend
Jerusalem; defending also He will deliver it; passing
over He will preserve it." (Isaiah 31:5)

These final battles against evil are symbolized as a "Marriage supper of the Lord". The "Fowls, the birds flying" are all
the symbol of God's power. What does the Hebrew Kabalic
philosophy say symbolizes God's power? The Hermes Bird,
the astrological Eagle-Scorpio, the Chinese Phoenix!

One more thing – the enemy and his filth are always symbolized in the Bible as the "generation of vipers" – the Serpent.

The Chinese Phoenix is therefore the emblem of the marriage fight of God for His people – which is the real significance when the Chinese associated this paired
Phoenix-dragon with marriage. The hero fights for his bride.
The ancient Chinese may have known the ancient prophecy

of the coming marriage of God with His people where the "Fowls and flying birds" will destroy the enemy, the Serpent, and his filth.

So, the southern constellation Scorpio represents the struggles against the Serpent which tries to seize the supreme Crown of Libra! And the mortal enemy of the Serpent is the noble Eagle alias Phoenix.

PHOENIX SAYINGS

There are several sayings which reflect the noble elegance and virtue of the Phoenix:

On Greatness

- There is the *Feng Huang* among men: Comparing men and referring to one who rises above them.
- A hen's nest does not give a Phoenix: Great things do not come from small things.
- The *luan* and Phoenix do not roost on thorny bushes: Great man in a small position.
- Dragon gall and Phoenix marrow: Rare ability.
- Born of a Dragon and reared by a Phoenix: Of royal birth. Used formerly of the Emperor.
- A rising dragon and a soaring Phoenix: A rising man or great scholar.
- Phoenix singing on high ridges: Deeds of great men are different from those lower.

On Happiness

- Phoenix without *wu-tung* tree and bamboo fruit will not eat: Without virtue you cannot get the best (also: No *wu-tung* tree the Phoenix will not come).
- Family with *wu-tung* tree will attract the Phoenix: Virtue brings happiness.

- Plant bamboo before the hall for the Phoenix and have a pond of fishes for dragons: Have the best.

On Marriage

- Seek a Phoenix without success: Trying in vain to get married.
- Male and female Phoenixes flying and singing together in concert: Harmonious marriage.

On Timing And Opportunity

- The Phoenix does not leave its perch: A man should confine himself to his sphere.
- Phoenix does not roost except on bamboo, wolf on *pei*: Mutual co-operation is necessary for the best work.
- Brindled cat in high spirit acts like tiger; a Phoenix in wrong time is not the equal of a chicken: There is a propitious time for everything.
- Male Phoenix sings towards the sun: Understanding what is obscure to others.

On Others

- Cooking a dragon and killing a Phoenix: A great feast.

THE CHINESE DRAGON

Linked with: Crocodile

The majestic creature with its bearded horned head and fish-tail and its four limbs with eagle claws threading the clouds and riding the foams of the seas, chasing that flaming pearl; that is the striking image of the Chinese *Lung* (Figure 5.1). *Lung*, the mythological Heraldic creature of the East, is misleadingly called the 'dragon' by westerners.

The *Lung* is the symbol of ancient China. The lores on the *Lung* are endless. The Chinese saying goes:

"Good fortune in the Dragon-Phoenix"

The Chinese Emperor is *Lung* seating on the *Lung* throne and wearing the *Lung* robes of gold. In Chinese philosophy, the *Lung* is the symbol of the Great Man. In Chinese *Feng-Shui* the energy forces affecting human destiny are "dragon lines". The *Lung* occupies important central meanings in the ancient Chinese culture. Thus, in the east, *Lung* is a venerated creature and harbinger of blessings.

In the west the 'dragon' seems to be an evil creature and the very incarnation of Satan (Seiss, 1972, p.58):

A most famous mythological creation of human thought is the terrible serpentine monster known as the dragon. With the serpent and others of the same repulsive and dangerous class, it is the universal symbol of evil ... The Serpent stands for that Evil One characterized by artifice, cunning, deceit and malignant subtlety. The Dragon stands for the same armed defiant power, putting forth imperial forms and devastating by force. The Serpent is the creeping sly deceiver, gliding smoothly to betray, insinuating his poison and destroying by stealth. The Dragon is the terrific oppressor, ... rushing vehemently and malignantly upon its prey. The Serpent and the Dragon are the same one, different only in manifestation. So, the Devil is called "the Dragon, that old Serpent".

Figure 5.2 illustrates several pictures of *Lung* through the ancient Chinese historical periods. The Shang Dynasty's *Lung* is viewed as a Double-Horned, Two-Limbed Fish-tailed non-serpentine being, alike to a half-man, half-fish. It is around the Han dynasty that the *Lung* begins to assume the traditional image of a Doubled-horned bearded, Four-limbed Fish-tailed serpentine creature.

Inscriptions of the word for *Lung* appeared on the Shang oracle bones (Hsu and Ward, 1984), placing the *Lung* in the very beginning of Chinese civilization in China around 1400BC. The Shang graph for *Lung* appears on the oracle bone as the name of a state (Hsu and Ward, 1984, p.459). The *Lung* was part of ancient Shang ceremonies:

Will there be rain if a *Lung* is constructed in a field?
(Shang oracle bone)

This custom of praying to the Dragon and placing a Dragon statute in the rice field still exist in Japan today (Hsu and Ward, 1984, p.462).

In 513BC, Duke Chao of Lu (in his 29th year of rule) noted a man in the time of Emperor Shun known as Tung-Fu who was fond of dragons and reared them. Consequently Emperor Shun conferred on the man the name Tung and his clan the name Huan-Tung. The Duke also noted that Kung-Chia of the Hsia Dynasty were given two teams of dragons by God, one team from the Ho River and the other from the Han. But

Kung-Chia was unable to feed and rear them until Liu Lei learnt the art from the Huan-Tung clan and helped Kung-Chia. These stories indicate that some amphibious animals might have been taken as *Lung*.

Figure 5.1: The Majestic Lung riding the clouds and threading the waves of the seas. It is the auspicious symbol of China and the Chinese Emperors–the symbol of Heavenly power conferred on Man.

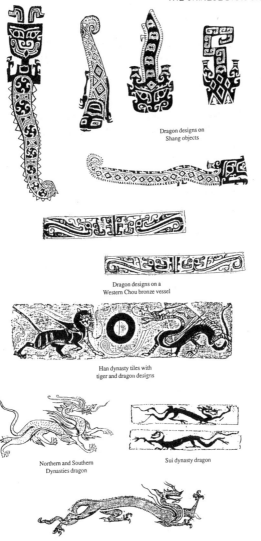

Dragon designs on
Shang objects

Dragon designs on a
Western Chou bronze vessel

Han dynasty tiles with
tiger and dragon designs

Northern and Southern
Dynasties dragon

Sui dynasty dragon

Five Dynasties dragon

Figure 5.2: Lung designs in various Chinese dynasties

DESCRIPTION OF LUNG

In the oldest form the *Lung* was a winged four-footed animal, each foot having four or five claws (Dennys, 1968, p.107). *Lung* is a composite image, its body representing various parts of nine different natural animals (Figure 5.1):

1. A head like a camel, with a pearl in his forehead, with a long beard, and with a sharp sword as a tongue. On each side of its mouth are whiskers, and a beard hangs under its chain, where a bright pearl is placed; Its breath proceeds from the mouth like a cloud; It changes into water or fire; Its voice is like the jingling of copper pans.

2. Horns of a deer,

3. Eyes of a rabbit,

4. Ears of a cow. It cannot hear, which is the reason deaf persons are called *lung*

5. Neck of a snake,

6. Belly of a frog,

7. Scales of a carp, as a ridge along its back, eighty-one in number; the scales on its throat lie towards the head, and those on the head are disposed like the ridges in a chain of mountains.

8. Legs and claws of a hawk, and

9. Palms of a tiger.

Lung is the chief among all animals which swim or crawl. It can be visible or invisible and assume all sorts of sizes. It ascends to heaven in spring and descends into the waters in autumn. It is not malicious nor poisonous like the Western dragon but is generally a benevolent creature particularly associated with bringing rains (Wu, 1982, p.5). Hence, *Lung* is not a natural animal known to Man, despite attempts to link it to giant lizards like the huge monitor lizards, crocodiles, alligators and Komodo Dragons.

The *Lung*, being a divine animal, dies of its own accord. It eats swallows' flesh, for which reason, when people pray to the Dragon for rain they throw swallows into the water. The Shou Wen dictionary, AD200 (William, 1931, pp.109-110) notes:

> *Lung* is the chief of the 369 species of scaly reptiles, such as fishes, snakes and lizards. It has the power of transformation and rendering itself visible or invisible at pleasure. It emerges and ascends to the skies in spring, and in autumn it buries itself in the watery depths and covers itself with mud; thus announcing by its awakening the return of nature's energies. It is naturally the symbol of productive force of moisture, that is of spring, when through genial rains and storms all nature renew itself.

Fossil remains of the Stegodon, Mastodon, Elephant and others are occasionally unearthed in various parts of North China. The bones are called Dragon's Bones and the fossil ivory is termed Dragon's Teeth; they are powdered, levigated and used medicinally in treatment of various ailments such as chorea, spermatorrhaea, ague and haemorrhages.

VARIETIES OF LUNG

There are horned and hornless *Lungs*, some are scaleless, and one kind has no wings. There is the Winged Dragon; the Coiling Dragon which inhabits the waters; and the Yellow Dragon which emerged from the River Lo to present the elements of writing to the legendary Emperor Fu-Hsi. The Winged *Lung* is the highest form of *Lung*. The Chinese cosmogonist has classified four chief kinds of *Lung*:

- Celestial Dragon *Tien Lung*, which guards and supports the mansions of the gods so that they would not fall;
- Spiritual Dragon *Shen Lung* which causes the wind to blow and produces rain for the benefit of mankind;
- *Ti Lung* of the earth, which marks out the courses of rivers and streams;
- *Lung* of the hidden treasures *Fu Tsang Lung* which watches over the wealth concealed from mortals eyes.

There are other chief fabulous species in the *Lung*'s group:

- *Lung* proper, which is most powerful and inhabits the sky
- *Li* which is hornless and lives in the ocean
- *Chiao* which is scaly and resides in marshes and mountains' dens. The *Chiao*, which inhabits the marshes and dens, differ but little from the *Lung* of the sky. It has a small head and neck, without horns, a breast of a crimson colour, a striped green and yellow sides back, has four legs, but is otherwise like a snake and about thirteen feet long."
- A primitive form akin to the *Lung* is known as *K'uei*. It is a beneficent creature, said to exert a restraining influence against the sin of greed, and it generally occurs in conventional form on ancient Chinese bronzes.

THE NINE OFFSHOOTS

According to legend, a certain *Lung* gave rise to nine distinct offshoots and they are respectively distinguished by special characteristics (Hsu and Ward, 1984, p.465). These creatures, according to the *Ch'ien Chu'eh Lei Shu* by Chen Jen-hsi are as follows:

1. *P'u lao*, carved on the tops of bells and gongs, reflecting its habit of crying out loudly when attacked by its archenemy the whale;

2. *Ch'iu niu*, carved on the screws of fiddles, for its taste for music;

3. *Pa-hsia*, carved on top of stone tablets, as it was fond of literature. It was said to represent a male and female tortoise bowing down with grief, and is largely used as a pedestal for tombstones, one head looking each way. It is a river god and is endowed with supernatural strength;

4. *Pu-hsia*, carved at the bottom of stone monuments, as it supports heavy weights;

5. *Chao-feng*, carved on the eaves of temples, reflecting its liking for danger;

6. *Chih-wen*, carved on the beams of bridges, owing to its fondness for water. It was placed on the roofs of buildings to keep off fire. It likes to gaze and look out and is thus symbolized by the figure of a fish with uplifted tail;

7. *Suan-ni*, carved on the Buddha's throne, for its propensity for resting. It is identified with the *Shih tzu* or symbolic lion;

8. *Yai tzu*, carved on sword-hilts, because of its lust for slaughter;

9. *Pi-kan*, carved on prison gates, for it likes litigation, quarrelling and use of its energy and strength, being very fierce. A scaly beast with one horn.

There must be some links between these "nine offsprings" of the *Lung* and the "nine animals" whose parts compose the *Lung*. These links could be the symbolism of the original division, reputedly by Emperor Yu, of ancient China into nine provinces (Gorn, 1902). This ancient event must have been so significant that its symbolism links with the number "Nine" which took several forms in Chinese memory.

Slightly different descriptions of *Lung* are given in the *Sheng An Wai Chi*, and other publications, which also mention the *Chiao-t'u* carved on door-handles as it likes to close things; the *T'ao-t'ieh*, carved on covers and sides of food-vessels as a warning against its gluttonous nature. There is the *Cha-yu* which has the head of a *Lung*, tail of a horse and claws of a tiger; this monster is 4 chang (40 feet) long, and loves to eat men; it appears in the world if the ruling sovereign shows a lack of virtue. Other relatives of the *Lung* may include the *Lang-pei* which is amphibious and has short hind legs that are unsuitable for movement. It rides upon other species which have long fore legs. This combination is a symbol of two persons joined together for evil purposes (William, 1931, p.112).

THE CROCODILE THEORY

The *Lung* was known in China from very ancient times. Its link with water leads to speculations to connect its real origins with some water animals. In fact, a Shang bronze wine mixer has a Yangtze Alligator together with a *Lung* design (Figure 5.3). This may seem to support the theory that some kind of similar reptile was taken as a common representation of the *Lung*. These ancient descriptions reflect thoughts of *Lung* as allied to the Crocodile:

- The *Lung* of the earth *Ti Lung*, which marks out the courses of rivers and streams;
- *Chiao* which is scaly and resides in marshes and dens in the mountains.

The Crocodile, in the animal symbolism of the Ganzhi's Twenty-eight Constellations, is also called *Ti Lung* or Earth Dragon (Table 2.3). The Crocodile perhaps comes closest but is still not exactly alike the physical looks of *Lung*; for William (1931, p.109) notes:

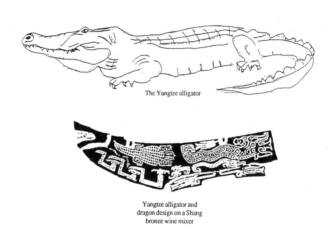

The Yangtze alligator

Yangtze alligator and
dragon design on a Shang
bronze wine mixer

Figure 5.3 : The Alligator and the Lung.
Many commentators have attempted to link the Lung with the
Yangtze alligator.

The crocodile was worshipped by the ancient Egyptians, and one theory is that the Chinese *Lung* is a form of the alligator found occasionally in Yangtze River, for the emergence of the latter from hibernation synchronizes with the coming of spring, the time of *Lung*'s beneficent influence. However, it is difficult to trace this fabulous animal to any natural species, for the body of this *Lung* seems serpentine, its head with parts of various other animals, the teeth are those of a mammalian carnivore, while the legs and claws are those of a bird.

Lung is capable of flying. This amphibious creature may be one which could fly; though modern science would know of no such natural creature. Hsu and Ward (1984) postulate that the *Lung* is related not only to the Yangtze Alligator but also the tornado and rains which come coinciding with the appearance of the river alligator. *Lung* is thus regarded as a merging of the Alligator with the features of the accompanying rains and tornado; therefore the flying part.

It has also been postulated that *Lung*, whose beneficial influences centre around water, is a symbol of the Hwang-Ho River. This river is the cradle of Chinese civilization and its waters are so important to the crops feeding the millions of people. Hence, the sinuous river is revered in the form of *Lung*. This theory, however, merely reflects the characteristic of only one of the four types of *Lung*:

> The *Lung* of the earth *Ti Lung*, which marks out the courses of rivers and streams.

The above different interpretations may all be correct as they show *Lung* have several layers of significance, of which the well-known water-regulating roles compose merely one facet. The ancient origins of the *Lung* must be related to more fundamental event(s) which accounts also of other significance of the *Lung*, like the association with divine power, the Emperor and roles of "guardian of sacred things".

AUSPICIOUS MEANINGS OF LUNG

China is the home of dragon worship. *Lung* is basically a benevolent being whose auspicious influence would be summed up by the following Chinese saying:

"Good fortune in the *Lung*-Phoenix"

In the East the *Lung* is a venerated being and harbinger of blessings. It is not malicious nor poisonous but is generally a benevolent creature particularly associated with bringing rains (Wu, 1982, p.5).

There are several other layers of significance of *Lung* in the Chinese culture:

- The *Lung* is distinctly the Imperial symbol of ancient China and the Chinese Emperor. The Imperial significance is often associated with "Nine *Lungs*" which are motifs worn on Imperial robes.
- In Chinese philosophy, like in the *I Ching*, the *Lung* is the symbol of the Great Man.
- The *Lung* represents the benevolent influences of water in the forms of rivers and rains.
- The *Lung*, particularly the Double Dragons (Figure 5.4), reflects the "Guardian" power of angels watching over the Universe and Man.
- In Chinese *Feng-Shui* the energy forces affecting human destiny are called "dragon lines". The *Lung* occupies important central meanings in the ancient Chinese religious culture.

Lung is the essence of strength, goodness and blessings. The *Lung* is a righteous being. Though it gives prosperity and happiness to the people, within its mouth there is also a sword ready to strike at a moment's notice when there has been an offence against Heaven.

Several sayings reflecting the auspicious meanings of the *Lung* are given in Table 5.1. Only one other symbol may also sum up the essence of the Chinese culture: this is the Eight Diagrams or Pakua.

Figure 5.4: The Double Lungs.
Often placed on either side of the main doors. The Double Lungs
are another representation of the two Door Gods and thus
symbolize protection against evil.

Table 5.1

Dragon Sayings

As the *Lung* is a royal powerful creature, there are several sayings associating it to great things and personages:

- Dragon Prince: Very rich and elegant person.
- The Dragon's presence, not water depth, makes the water effective: Reputation of a place depends on its men not its size.
- Dragon coiled and Tiger ready to spring: Impregnable position.
- Dragon is chief of the Four Spiritual Animals: The leader (also Dragon is chief of scaly animals).
- Rising Dragon and soaring Phoenix: An upcoming man.
- Dragon' steps and tiger's gaze: Dignified (also Dragon's walk and tiger's pace).
- Dragon flying in the sky: One who has won power.
- Dragon among men: A famous man.
- A pen moving as Dragon and Snake: Exquisite penmanship.
- Dragon-Tiger list: List of successful examination candidates.
- Soil God eats earthworms; that which one loves is a Golden Dragon: Precious.
- Some dragon sayings signify auspicious times: Dragon's breath becomes clouds.
- Dragon returns to sea caves, clouds retain their moisture; the grass and trees retain their perfume; musk deer crosses the green hills.
- Man relies on Dragon King; Tiger on the mountain; wife on the husband: Each has something to depend on.
- Dragon bringing water: Raining.
- Nine Dragons playing in water: About to rain.

LUNG AS THE IMAGE OF WATER

Lung represents the beneficent influences of water and its multiple forms including the clouds and even winds and waterspouts. *Lung* is said to have the power to raise huge waves to injure men and boats. The popular Dragon Boat Festival on the 5th day of the 5th month reflects the influence of *Lung* in providing water. Storms are regarded as the results of the swirling activities of the *Lung*.

The ancient East depicts the dragon as possessing life-giving powers through the agency of water. In most ancient concepts the dragon controls water on earth in the forms of rivers, streams, seas, pools, wells; and in the sky in the forms of clouds, thunder and lightning. It is essentially life-giving and is venerated even though it has its angry menacing moods in storms.

The many manifestations of storm clouds are the moving *Lung*. Lightning forks are the claws of the *Lung*. Its voice is like thunder in the winds which scatter the withered forest leaves and renew the spring. The *Lung* signifies the essence of flux and change, therefore of life itself.

Shen Lung, the Divine *Lung*, regulates the streams, floods, seas and rains, and can be a blessing or a curse to man. He moves his head and blows out the clouds that the earth may nourished. At other times he returns to his sea home and the clouds retain their moisture. During a drought he is most earnestly sought by all classes of the people. It is to him that the people must look for the rains which give the harvests, he is considered man's friend. He constantly does things for which the people should bless him.

On the other hand, he is blamed for the floods, obstructed rivers, and many of the cataclysms of nature.

FENG-SHUI AUSPICIOUSNESS OF LUNG

The *Lung* also exerts its benevolence through means other than water.

Lung is the very essence of vitality. Every hill and river seems to be inhabited by dragons and when a house is built the *Feng-Shui* master would be consulted about the dragon spirits. The house shrine for the house deity is put up for the local dragon which will help protect the precincts of the family house. The virtue of the house dragon lasts about one hundred years when the powers of the dragon need to be reinvigorated with more elaborate ceremonies. Three days are spent in preparations and on the fourth day the exorcism of evil influences is carried out. He would then go to the nearest hill and invoke the dragon spirit to return.

He exerts his power in protecting the places of those he likes from evil influences and demons. For this reason any spot where he will dwell in peace is fortunate. But when he is not permitted to live in his chosen home, he becomes a menace to the community. He may be either a friend or an enemy of man, as he chooses.

ASSOCIATION OF DRAGONS
WITH CHINESE EMPERORS

Lung is the Imperial symbol of themselves, the Emperor. The types of dragons reflect the rank of the royalty:

1. A Five-clawed dragon is the emblem of the Emperor, his sons and princes of first and second ranks.

2. A Four-clawed dragon is the emblem of princes of third and fourth ranks.

3. Princes of fifth rank and certain officials could use a serpent-like creature with five claws.

Why is the *Lung* the symbol of the Chinese Emperor? The Emperor is especially associated with the "Nine *Lungs* motif, which is embroidered onto the Emperor's robes and are also cast onto the wall screens in the Imperial palace. Why nine *Lungs* and not ten or five?

Nine is also the number of several auspicious things of ancient China. Is this number ever associated with the emperor? Yes, in the Nine Emperor Gods. The Nine Emperor Gods are believed to be the long-life first nine human sovereigns who lived in antediluvian times and came after nonhuman rulers (Cheu, 1988; Hirth, 1908). They are really Chinese memory of the nine antediluvian and long-life patriarchs of the Bible from Adam to Lamech, the father of Noah. Therefore, Nine *Lungs* are the symbol of the antediluvian Nine Emperor Gods which the Middle East knew as the nine Biblical patriarchs before the Flood.

The Emperor was not only the sovereign of the nation, but he was also the high priest of the nation, offering the annual sacrifices to Shang-Ti, the Supreme God (Bilsky 1975). The very Chinese character for ruler *Wang* depicts the sacrificial fire on the ground and denotes the priest. But during those ancient times, even in many ancient cultures, the priests were often the rulers!

The etymology of the ancient oracle bone script for *Lung* shows *Lung* originally is not an animal but a man! (Figure 5.5). This man appears to have a halo around his head which is the result of his standing before the sacrificial fire. He also wears a long sash which has been mistaken for the dragon's tail. The ancient word *Lung* actually denotes a priest-king! *Lung* therefore represents the emperor who was the priest-king of ancient China. Of the humans closest to God during those times, the *Lung* denotes the highest human being – the priest-king! Hence, the Chinese emperor appropriated the *Lung* as his Imperial symbol.

| Oracle Bone 14-11 c BC | Bronze 11-3 c BC | Small Seal 3 c BC | Li-shu | Modern (K'ai-shu) |

LUNG
dragon,
emblem of
imperialism

YU
fish

KUEI (GUI)
tortoise

Figure 5.5: The words "Lung", "Fish" and "Tortoise".

As the symbol of the Emperor as the Priest of God, *Lung* is related to the winged-with-hands holy *seraphim* of God in the Bible and the Jewish Kabalic philosophy:

> Above it stood the *seraphim* [8314]: Each has six wings; with twain he covered his face and with twain he covered his feet and with twain he did fly. And one cried unto another and said, Holy, holy, holy is the Lord of hosts; the whole earth is full of his glory ... (Isaiah 6:2-3)

> Then flew one of the seraphim [8314] unto me, having a live coal in his hand which he had taken with the tongs from the altar ... Lo, this hath touched thy lips and thine iniquity is taken away and thy sin purged. (Isaiah 6:6-7)

The *seraphim* are creatures associated with the process of purging sins. The *seraphim* are priest-like creatures! *Seraphim* are associated with priest functions. That is, the *Seraphim-Lung* symbol of the Chinese Emperor denotes his role as a priest-king who dealt and took away the sins of his people through the Imperial worship of Shang-Ti, the Supreme God. When Huang-Ti is called the Yellow Emperor he is also associated with the central Yellow Dragon. Fu-Hsi (the Biblical Adam) is called the Azure Dragon of the East – Adam who was apparently driven eastward from the Garden of Eden. The Chinese Emperors were always the priest-kings of their nation.

Lung is the symbol of the Emperor as God's Priest-King.

RELATED AUSPICIOUSNESS
IN OTHER CULTURES

Earlier, it has been discussed that the Four Heraldic Animals is not unique to ancient China but is also found in other ancient Middle East cultures (Chapter 3).

The Dragon does not arise independently in various civilizations but has a common origin probably in the ancient Sumerian civilization which may have derived its ideas from or passed them to Egypt. An earliest representation of dragons is on an archaic cylinder-seal from Susa and depicts a lion or lioness combined with an eagle or falcon. The ancient Chinese dragon is more complicated, with camel head, deer horns, ox ears, elephant tusks, serpentine body, fish scales, ridge-shaped horny spine, long serpentine fish-tail, four legs with feet of tiger and eagle claws (Whittick, 1960, pp.176-178).

As the beneficent life-giving element of water, *Lung* is the national symbol of Imperial China and emblem of the Japanese Emperor. The Romans adopt it as their standard (along with the eagle) and it also appeared as the emblem of English-Welsh kings like Henry VII, Henry VIII, James I. The dragon was also the emblem of the West Saxons. The dragon is further represented as a guardian of treasure. The golden apples of Hesperides Garden were guarded by Ladon, the hundred-headed dragon (Whittick, 1960, pp.176-178).

While the Dragon is a benevolent creature in several cultures, it was only in the Bible that the Dragon was associated with the evil Serpent (Whittick, 1960, pp.177-178). It appears that Indian Buddhism introduced some confusion, for the Lamas and Chinese Buddhists, not daring to call the mythical Indian Serpents (*Naga*) serpents as what they really are, termed these Nagas as *Lung* in their translations of the Sanskrit Buddhist scriptures (Williams, 1931, p.109).

ASTROLOGICAL SIGNIFICANCE OF LUNG

Lung is the fifth of the Zodiacal Animals and its astrological characteristics are illustrated in Table 5.2.

Table 5.2

The Terrestrial Branch Significance Of Lung

Order of Animals:	5th
Time ruled by:	*Lung* 5th Hour, Ch'en (0700 to 0900)
Season:	End of Spring
Month:	5th astronomical moon
Direction:	S60E
Western Constellation:	Aries
Ruling Planet:	Mars
Lucky Gemstone:	Amethyst
Shade:	Yang
Year:	1904, 1916, 1928, 1940, 1952, 1964, 1976, 1988
Associated Immortal:	Fu-Hsi (Azure *Lung*), Huang-Ti (Golden *Lung*)
Symbol:	Good augury and luck. Also symbolizes powers of destiny.
Good points:	Determined, strong, fighter. Not cunning or guileful. Lively, full of vitality Follow own judgement but just and magnanimous. Admired, highly intelligent. Filial.
Bad points:	Seldom agree with elders, Blunt and rough, Risk mistakes from error of judgement. Eccentric and egoistic.
Others:	Can succeed if check his impulses and improve his ways.
Compatible:	Monkey, Rat, Snake
Incompatible:	Ox, Dog.

These features are those of the Ten Celestial Stems level.

In Chinese *Feng-Shui*, *Lung* is the East of the Four Animals of the Four Cardinal Directions (Figure 2.6, 3.1). *Lung* has two different sets of significance as it represents not only the 5th of the Zodiac Animals, but also one of the Four Heraldic Animals of the Four Directions:

1. **Ten Celestial Stems**

   These are the Five Elements of Wood, Fire, Metal, Water and Earth. They are also represented by the Four Heraldic Animals of *Lung* at East, Phoenix at South, Tiger at West and Snake-Tortoise at North, with the central Earth position occupied by another *Lung* – the Golden *Lung*.

   They are essentially the highest angels controlling the four spheres of Heaven. Each of the Four Heraldic Animals also appears to have under each seven other animals, forming the Twenty-Eight Constellations.

2. **Twelve Terrestrial Branches**

   They are the Twelve Zodiac Animals, including the *Lung* or the 12 years in the Jupiter Cycle. They could also represent the twelve points of the compass as well as the twelve divisions of the day and year.

   They are the twelve areas of angelic influences on Earth.

   The Celestial Stems are the angelic forces of Heaven, while the Terrestrial Branches are the angelic forces on Earth – their interactions, as postulated by the Ganzhi System, regulates the whole Universe. Hence, the *Lung* would have a set of meanings associated with the Heavenly *Lung* and another set of meanings associated with the Earthly *Lung*.

Most of the beneficial influences and auspiciousness ascribed to *Lung* are those of the Celestial Stems level. That is, they represent the powers and manifestations of the Heavenly *Lung*. The Zodiac *Lung* is really the characteristic of the terrestrial guardian angel of the man it is associated with – hence its attributes are terrestrial and may determine major features of the behaviour and hence destiny of the man born under the *Lung* sign.

The significance of *Lung* at the Ten Celestial Stems level is summarized in Table 5.3. The *Lung* also forms two of these Twenty-Eight Constellations under the East *Lung*:

- Earth Dragon (sometimes known as Crocodile) is the first lunar constellation of Chiao the Horn, a cross-like four stars in Virgo. The *Tong-Shu* says: Building on this day will bring glory and prosperity. Educated men will be able to approach the Emperor. Marriages on this day give numerous progenies. Repairing a tomb or attending a funeral this day brings grief.

- Sky Dragon is the second lunar constellation of Kang the Neck, four stars in the feet of Virgo. The *Tong-Shu* says: Building this day causes the eldest not to succeed. Doing things the next ten days will be disastrous. Funerals and marriages will cause untimely death and make widows.

LUNG MEN, THE DRAGON GATE

One of the marvellous richness of the Chinese imagination is that various creatures could hope to develop into *Lung*. There are also other methods of attaining dragonhood. Both the Snake and the Fish through patient exertion and much suffering may ascend to this exalted state. However, this is accomplished only through a long period during which their acts have always been for the good of the world.

One of the popular motifs of creatures becoming a *Lung* is that of the Carp leaping over the Dragon Gate (Figure 5.6): "The carp leaps the dragon gate" i.e. to gain a degree.

The *Lung Men* (Dragon Gate) is a cataract of the Yellow River in Ho Ching district in Shansi. The fish goes up the river and one which leap the barrier becomes dragons. Their tails are burned off by lightning as they go over it. Those that do not succeed fall on the rocks and die or thunder kills them.

The few who escape have marks left on their foreheads. There are a number of other places called the Dragon Gate.

Figure 5.6: Carp leaping across "Lung-Men" (Dragon Gate). Leaping across the "Lung-Men", which is the cataract along the Yellow River, signifies success in academic studies. The ancient Chinese knew that literary success often means automatic assurance of position and wealth.

The sea-Serpent, after a period of five hundred years becomes a scaly Dragon, after another one thousand years he becomes a hornless Dragon. After another five hundred years he may become a horned Dragon. Again after a period of a thousand years he may become a winged Dragon. A number of sayings encourage people to be diligent, in imitation of the Fish striving to become a Dragon:

- Fish becomes Dragon: Success in literary examination.
- Carp leaps the Dragon's Gate.
- Man of ability may leap the Dragon Gate.
- Once the Dragon Gate was scaled one's reputation increases tenfold.
- Dragon leaps the celestial gate: Rise to a very high position.
- Bamboo sprouts shed sheath; fish tossed by waves will become dragons: No perfection without trials.

AUSPICIOUS LEGENDS OF LUNG

Stories about *Lung* in Chinese folklores are many and among the richest and most colourful. However, two significant legends which play tremendous roles in Chinese culture are the Dragon Boat Festival and Tang Emperor Taizong and the Dragon King.

TANG EMPEROR TAIZONG
AND THE DRAGON KING

The story of the Tang Emperor Taizong and the Dragon King is a well-known story elaborated in the story of the Monkey God in *Journey to the West* (Wu Cheng'en, Ming dynasty).

During the Tang dynasty, the dragon god of rain wanted to show that a fortune-teller was wrong about being able to predict things. The Dragon King thought he could confound the fortune-teller by making him predict about the time, location and the amount of rainfall. The Dragon King set to scatter rain according to its own liking despite the fact that a messenger from Heaven announced the Supreme God's instructions about the rain just as the fortune-teller foretold.

The Dragon King's disobedience to the instructions of the Supreme God was a serious offence and the heavenly prime minister was to behead him at a specific time. The dragon appeared to the Tang Emperor Taizong in a dream and begged the Emperor to influence the minister Wei Zheng to save him. The Emperor called up the minister and purposely played chess with the prime minister hoping to make him forget the time and thus save the dragon. The minister was tired and went to sleep. But he suddenly woke up and cried that he had to do a beheading. The dragon's head fell from the sky and drop right between them.

The dragon's ghost appeared to the Emperor and threatened him for breach of promise and insisted on bringing up the case in the netherworld. The Emperor fell sick as the haunting came every night. Eventually, the generals agreed to take turns to guard the Emperor's front doors. The demon did not come and the Emperor slept peacefully. This is the origin of custom of placing the Door Gods. In some cases these two Door Gods are replaced by two Dragons ornamented onto the doors!

But the Emperor's condition deteriorated. The minister Wei Zheng then devised a scheme whereby the Emperor when his soul was in Hell would obtain the help of Hell Judge Cui, one of Wei Zheng's friends in Hell, to save the Emperor. Judge Cui resolved the case in favour of the Emperor as it was written in the books of Fate that the Dragon King was destined then to die at the hands of a personal minister.

The Emperor begged forgiveness and made a new promise to the Dragon King. The Emperor instructed that a place of honour be given to the dragon by having the officers and the people to carry the dragon above their heads. The dragon's head was also placed on every palace's roof and thus the origin of the dragon on the roofs of temples.

The two generals of Emperor Taizong are well-known Door Gods in the ancient Chinese culture. They are older than the Tang dynasty but have been appropriated into the story of *Journey to the West*. The same Door Gods could be replaced by the Double Dragons (Figure 5.4).

These Door Gods are also connected to the ancient New Year Eve's custom of putting up the red coloured cloths at the door to ward off evil. The dragon's ghost which haunted the Emperor Taizong is depicted in the legend of the Nien Dragon-Beast which comes at New Year Eve. During this time the dragon's ghost is scared off with firecrackers and the red cloths at the door.

DRAGON BOAT FESTIVAL

The Fifth Month Festival or Summer Festival or Dragon Boat Festival is one of the three main folk festivals of China. The others being the Spring Festival and the Mid-Autumn Festival.

The popular Dragon Boat Festival is held on the 5th day of the 5th moon. On this day, long narrow boats, holding as many as sixty or more rowers, race up and down the river in pairs with much clamour, as if searching for someone who has been drowned. The dragon boat is generally a long narrow boat, measuring about 120 feet in length, $2\frac{1}{2}$ feet in depth, and $5\frac{1}{2}$ feet in width. The bow of the boat is ornamented or carved with a dragon's head, and the stern with a dragon's tail, and carries men beating gongs and drums and waving flags to inspire the rowers with renewed exertions on their rowing. Accidents frequently occur during these races and the local authorities in some district have accordingly restricted or forbidden this practice.

The festival is popularly believed to have been instituted in memory of a statesman poet named Ch'u Yuan (332-296BC) a native of Ying who drowned himself in the River Mi-lo in 295BC, after having been falsely accused by one of the petty princes of the state, and as a protest against the corrupt condition of the government. During the Warring States Period some 2,300 years ago Ch'u Yuan was born in the State of Chu in the southern part of China at a time when Chinese society was in the throes of cataclysm. He frowned upon the corruptness of the aristocrats in the state. The people, who loved the unfortunate courtier for his virtue and fidelity sent out boats in search of the body, but to no purpose. They then prepared a peculiar kind of rice called *tsung* made of glutinous rice wrapped in leaves. Several of these were placed on the spot of the tragedy to be sacrificed to the spirit of the loyal statesman, Ch'u Yuan. This mode of commemorating the event has been carried down to posterity as an annual holiday.

It was also possible that this festival had an earlier origin, and was inaugurated with the object of propitiating the beneficent dragon, in the hope that he would send down sufficient rain for the crops (Williams, 1931, p.114).

The Fifth Month Festival had long been observed before the birth of Ch'u Yuan and the many customs observed on that day had something to do with Dragon. The glutinous rice wrapped up in reed leaves during the Dragon Boat Festival was originally offered as a sacrifice to the Dragon. In those days it was customary to collect rain water on that day which was supposed to be the holy water spread on earth by the heavenly dragon and this water was said to have the reputation of preventing diseases. In some places in ancient times, bronze mirrors with designs of crouched dragons on them were cast into a river. With these mirrors on hand, rain would come if one prayed to heaven for it (Xing, 1988, pp.36-37).

Despite the gaiety of the Dragon Boat Festival, the 5th Day of the 5th moon is generally known as the most evil day in the year. It is the Summer Solstice, the longest day; after which the days become shorter.

The date of the Dragon Boat Festival is also the date when the Taoist Pope Chang Tao-Ling would ride out on his Tiger to quell the demons. This date is also the date when the paper charm with the Eight Diagrams above the five poisonous animals is placed on roofs against evil influence. Artemesia would be put out on the 5th day of the 5th month to ward off evil.

Eberhardt (1972) points out that there is evidence that Ch'u Yuan was a member of the Tai tribe as his poems contain elements of Tai ceremonial and sacrificial songs. The 5th Day of the 5th Moon is a Tai day for human sacrifice. Hence, Ch'u Yuan's suicide could be a self-human sacrifice. In fact, the boat races of the Dragon Boat Festival compose an ancient method of choosing a human sacrifice, as some boats would overturn and some men would be drowned.

It appears indeed that the 5th Day of the 5th Moon, associated with the Dragon Boat Festival, was an ancient memory of some ancient event carried out to drive away evil.

Appendix

THE CHINESE CHARACTER FOR LUNG

There are some tendencies to confuse *Lung* with Snakes. In the Heraldic arrangement the Chinese *Lung* at the East is a different creature from the Snake at the North; which should be a warning not to confuse the *Lung* with a Snake. These two classes of animals are different.

Look at forms of the Chinese character for *Lung* (Figure 5.7):

A. LUNG, "DRAGON"

Vapour and clouds personified, giving rise to rains when it flies in heaven and causes drought when it hides in wells. The ancient word is pictorial. The modern word: "Fei" on right, contracted wings; "Li" on right, top, believed to be contraction of "Tung" for heavy and used as phonetic with "Ju" on right, bottom for body.

B. SHE, "SNAKE"

Composes of "Hui" and "To", see below. It particularly refers to the Serpent or Cobra.

HUI refers to crawling creatures such as snakes, worms.

T'O the Snake standing on its tails with the tongue darting out.

Figure 5.7: Fundamental subcharacters of "Lung" and "She"

Lung, the dragon. When it ascends to fly in heaven, it rains. When it hides in the wells, there is drought. It is vapours and clouds personified. The ancient form is a recognizable representation. The modern form is interpreted as: to the right, *Fei* (fly) contracted, the wings; to the left bottom *Ju* or *Jou* (pieces of dry meat) the body; left top, *li* thought to be *Tung* contracted, a phonetic (after Weiger, 1965, p.309, Lesson 140)

Dragon. The last right symbol is a fanciful sketch of the fabulous creature. The middle symbol which is similar to the modern one; its right component seems to be a contraction of *Fei* to fly (symbolizing the dragon's wings), the lower left part (*Jou*) is the body and its upper part (*Li*) is a contraction of *Tung* heavy (after Vaccari and Vaccari, 1950, p.58).

Both Weiger (1965) and Vaccari and Vaccari (1950) recognize the winged nature of the Chinese *Lung*. Figure 5.7 besides showing the 'wings' also shows that the pictorial form of Chinese *Lung* has:

1. four protrusions on the top of the head – likely representing the horns

2. and four limbs

In order to emphasize further the difference between the Chinese *Lung* and the serpent we should study the Chinese character for serpent. Figure 5.7 shows the Chinese character forms for *She* the serpent (Weiger, 1965, p.259, lesson 108 and p.261, lesson 110A). *She* for serpent is formed from *Hui* for crawling and *To* for snake. The pictorial representation for *To* shows the typical hissing tongue of the snake while *Hui* shows its crawling form. There are no limbs, wings and horns to the *She* serpent. The Chinese *She* serpent is definitely not *Lung*!

The Chinese characters show that *Lung* is limbed, winged and horned; unlike the limbless *She* serpent.

Although Chinese illustrations often do not show wings on the *Lung*, the Chinese *Lung* is by implication a winged creature:

"There are several varieties; some are horned and others hornless, some are scaleless, and one kind has no wings ... Celestial Dragon ... Spiritual Dragon ... Winged Dragon ... Horned Dragon ... Coiling Dragon ... Yellow Dragon ... "

Actually the Chinese Winged Dragon is the highest of the order of Dragons.

6

THE SNAKE

Linked with: Tortoise

The image of the Snake (Figure 6.1) would trigger off a host of negative impressions. One would be a common fear of the poisonous creature, whose venomous bite could be fatal. Some would shrink back at its slithery feel. The uncomfortable feeling that the Snake heralds impending darkness and evil repulses people from the Snake.

The fear of Snakes as poisonous is not accurate as only a few species are really venomous. In the Asian region the Cobra, Viper and Sea-snake are venomous. Some rare individuals would testify that Snakes make good pets!

Figure 5.7 illustrates the Chinese character for Snake. The character is a combination of two sub-characters namely, *ch'ung* on the left, meaning crawling creatures, and *t'o* on the right for a Snake "that stands on its tail distending its neck and darting its tongue out" (Weiger, 1950). The ancient and more pictorial representation shows the resemblance of the hood of the cobra clearly.

The legendary flying Serpent is the Cobra which seems to fly from its reared position when it darted forward to attack.

Despite its so-called evil aura, Snakes are worshipped at the San-chieh temples (also called *Ch'ing She Miao* or Green Serpent temples). The serpents would crawl out to eat or drink the offerings laid before the altar of the Snake God, Chor Choo-Kong, who was the embodiment of the Black Snake. Instead of using black which is an unlucky colour, the Chinese may resort a euphemism and call it Green Snake. The Snake God is a fierce god. If a person failed to keep his vow to the Snake God, there is nowhere he could flee – the Serpents would come after him relentlessly. Similar snake temples are found in Canton where the reptiles could be seen among the temple grounds. They do not disturb or harm the worshippers, possibly mesmerized by the smoke of the incense.

Figure 6.1: The Serpent.
Universal symbol of evil. The Chinese character "she" for the
snake is the venomous cobra.

These Snakes are supposed to hold in their heads various precious stones. The Serpent's flesh is attributed with several healing powers. The white spotted Snake skin is used in leprosy, rheumatism and palsy. Snakes are caught and sold as food, the poisonous ones used as medicines.

GENERAL INAUSPICIOUS MEANINGS
OF SNAKE

The Snake is a most feared animal among the creatures. The Snake, like the Dragon and Tiger, has two different sets of symbolism. One is due to its position in the Ten Celestial Stems as the Heraldic Animal of the North, the Black Snake, and the other is its position as the sixth animal of the Twelve Terrestrial Branches. Associated with the North, the Black Snake is a veritable symbol of disasters and all sorts of evil coming down from the North. In military operations, a superstitious general would try to attack the enemy from the North. If the general is to the South of the enemy he would make a detour north and attack from that direction. Otherwise, he would be fated to lose. For some reasons, the Black Snake could be replaced by the Black Tortoise or Dark Warrior as the Animal of the North.

The Snakes, like Foxes, appear as spirits or as lost souls of men and would return to old haunts. Evil spirits like demons, elves and fairies can assume the form of Snakes, while supernatural Serpents could manifest themselves as ordinary mortals.

The Serpent is the most common symbol of evil and the evil spirit, though it has also been said to symbolize wisdom and healing. Earliest Oriental, Greek and even Christian myths associated the monster Serpent or Dragon to the forces of evil. The St. George's Dragon is originally not a dragon but a great "worm", that is, a large Snake. The Indian god Brahma was often shown in sculptures to rise from the vanquished

Serpent. In Greek myth the Eagle carried the defeated Serpent. If it coiled around the tree it is the vivid symbol of temptation. Some Eastern people believe that immunity against the venomous Snakes could be propitiated through worship of them (Whittick, 1960, p.258).

The Indians said that a black Snake on the right side of the road is auspicious but not on the left. A white Snake anywhere is bad and should be killed. It is unlucky to kill a Snake which stays below the floor of one's house.

The Snake is classed as one of the Five Poisonous Animals, similar to the Scorpion, Centipede, Frog and Lizard, which denotes symbolism of evil influences especially on plagues and drought. A pot of Artemesia could be placed on the fifth day of the fifth month against them. The demon queller Ching Kuei could also be invoked during the last days of the fourth month as protection against them. His paper charms would be pasted onto the rafters of houses. Another deity who could be invoked against these Five Poisonous Animals is the Taoist Pope Chang Tao-Ling who likes to ride the Tiger on his excursions against evil, especially on the fifth day of the fifth month (q.v. Tiger). Note that this fifth day of the fifth month is also the Dragon Boat Festival (q.v. *Lung*). Love charms are most effective when made at this time. This love charm is called a *Ku* and is really a form of Snake spirit. The Centipede, the *jang-ho* plant (a form of wild ginger) and the lotus root are said to be antidotes against the *Ku* charm.

AUSPICIOUS MEANINGS OF SNAKE

The Serpent is also associated with the secrets of life and hence wisdom (Whittick, 1960, p.258). Essentially, this is derived from its symbol of sycophancy, cunning and evil and its supposed kinship to the majestic dragon.

It was venerated as a symbol of healing when Moses' brazen Serpent healed the Snake-bitten Israelites. The serpent symbol is found on the emblem of Asclepius god of medicine and of modern medicine (Whitticks, 1968, p.258). The followers of the western Esculapius and Hygia considered a coiled serpent around a staff as a symbol of health (Dennys, 1968, p.103). This figure of the Serpent has never been used in Chinese culture in this way. The Serpent may have been misleadingly taken as a symbol of healing as in Asclepius' wand which has a coiled Serpent(s) wand topped by a pair of wings (Figure 6.2). This depicts the Serpents being defeated by the Falcon symbolized by the pair of wings above the Serpents (q.v. Falcon). In truth the Asclepius' wand is the symbol of the healing power of the Falcon, not the Snake.

ASTROLOGICAL SIGNIFICANCE

The Snake seems to symbolize evil but what is its significance in the Twelve Zodiacal Animals System? Does the Snake signify evil here, too?

No. The reason is that much of the evil associated with the Snake is related to the *tiangan* Ten Celestial Stems significance. The *tiangan* position denotes its malevolent external extraterrestrial influence. By associating the Snake with the *dizhi* Twelve Terrestrial Branches, the other natural qualities of the Snake should be considered – that is, desirable qualities like its general industriousness and cunningness in reflecting the internal conditions of the earth and the inherent tendencies of the person born under this sign in the *dizhi* Twelve Terrestrial Branches system (Table 6.1).

There are two factors – i) a heavenly or non-earthly factor and; ii) an earth factor. Some seemingly double and conflicting symbolisms are due to this fact.

Figure 6.2: (Right) The Falcon – enemy of the snakes.
The Falcon swooping on the snakes is the actual symbolism of the Hermes Wand.
(Left) Hermes Trimegister the Messenger of goods, also known as the Biblical Enoch and the father of astrology, holds a winged wand with two snakes entwined. The Hermes Wand represents the Falcon swooping down on the snakes.

The Snake is also the twenty-seventh constellation, *I* or Wings. The *Tong-Shu* describes it as falling on a Tuesday under the influence of Mars and being inauspicious:

Building today will lead to successive deaths of the house masters. Funerals and marriages will not give prosperity. Young girls will run from home.

SYMBOLIC SNAKE LORE

Snakes and Fishes are creatures which after long periods of efforts could become Dragons. After five hundred years the serpent may become a Scaly Dragon; after another one thousand years a Hornless Dragon; after another five hundred years a Horned Dragon; finally after another one thousand years the Winged Dragon.

There are several Snake sayings:

Dragon's head, snake's tail: Great schemes which have small results.

A great dragon is no match for the local snake: At times a local familiar with his natural environment is more than a match for the stranger of greater ability.

The Snake is associated with the first female Nu Kua, the sister-consort of the first man, World First Emperor Fu-Hsi. She is also a Snake Goddess who repaired the heavens. However, there is a dispute whether Nu Kua has a snake body or a rear fish body with the fish-tail. In the later form, she may be depicted as a Dragon Lady.

One of the most tragic folk tales on Snakes is the story of Madam White Snake.

MADAM WHITE SNAKE

Madam White Snake or *Pai-she* was originally a huge white female Serpent who had been meditating for eighteen hundred years in the Cavern of the Winds at the Green Mountain near Ching-to-foo in Szechuan. In the cave were the strange and wondrous shrubs and flowers. Madame White Snake has never done any harm to any human being. It has acquired vast wisdom and supernatural powers. It could take the form of a beautiful woman named Pi-Cheu-Niang.

In beautiful Hangchow were the magnificent palaces and gardens of princes and nobles and the ancient temples. The garden of Prince Chow was especially beautiful but had been deserted after the prince's death. A black Serpent had resided in this garden for eight hundred years and had ascended from the clouds and changed into the form of a woman. The white Snake who was seeking a change of abode to increase her powers, came to this garden. The black Snake was reluctant to let it occupies the same garden. A contest was agreed upon where the defeated would be the servant of the victor. The black Snake used a sword to try to cut the white Snake. But the white Snake produced two swords and positioned them into a cross and she muttered a spell which overpowered the black Snake. The sword of the black Snake was snatched away and rendered her defenceless. She realized the superior powers of white Snake and knelt down, admitted defeat and she agreed to be the servant of the white Snake.

The two Snakes went into the world. Madam White Snake developed an unlucky attraction for a mortal. The enchantress brought grief to those connected to her.

According to Eberhard (1968, pp.399-402), this White Snake was Lin-shui fu-jen, the disciple of Master Hsu Chen-chun. She was a helper of women who wanted children and was also a protector of seamen. Master Hsu was a divine doctor, who defeated a *chiao* dragon which he imprisoned in the river water (this *chiao* spirit was also cast as a Snake from Mao-Shan Mountain, a place associated with Taoists who went there to learn black magic). The man who fell in love with Madam White Snake was a mortal named Hsu Han-wen or Hsu Hsien. This lover Hsu had a child by her. When he discovered his wife was a Snake he allowed a Buddhist monk to turn him against her. She was killed in the subsequent attempt to recover her husband.

There were some conflicting and confusing stories on this tale (Eberhard, 1968, pp.400-402). Some have linked the lover Hsu to Master Hsu, and that Master Hsu was the one who fought and killed Madam White Snake. Furthermore, some traditions linked *Pai-she* as the mother of the famous monk Hsuan-tsang of the *Journey to the West*. A bandit drowned his father Chen in the river and kidnapped his mother, who however, refused to make love with the bandit, a water *chiao* dragon spirit. The boy was brought up by the monks and later traced his mother and had the bandit killed. His father's body was kept by the fish-dragon was later restored to life.

Pai-she or Lin-shui fu-jen is also a *shui-hsien* (water deity) and is linked to the Goddess of Seafarers Ma-Tsu and Tien-Hou (Empress of Heaven), the latter of the same clan Lin as Lin-shui fu-jen. (Eberhard, 1968, p.402). In this tradition, she is also linked to the popular Goddess of Mercy Kuan-yin, who originally was also a seafarer deity.

TWENTY-EIGHT
CONSTELLATIONS SERIES

Azure Dragon:
1. Crocodile (22), Earth Dragon* (5),
2. Sky Dragon* (5),
3. Badger (23),
4. Hare* (14),
5. Fox (24),
6. Tiger* (8),
7. Leopard (25)

   Black Turtle:
8. Unicorn*, Griffon* (9),
9. Buffalo* (13),
10. Bat (26),
11. Rat* (12),
12. Swallow (27),
13. Pig* (20), Bear* (10),
14. Porcupine (28)

   White Tiger:
15. Wolf (29),
16 Dog* (19),
17. Pheasant (30),
18. Cock* (18),
19. Crow, Raven (31),
20. Monkey*,
21. Gibbon* (17)

   Red Phoenix:
22. Tapir (32),
23. Goat*, Sheep* (16),
24. Buck (33),
25. Horse* (15),
26. Stag (33),
27. Snake* (6),
28. Earthworms (34)

* covered in Heraldic or Zodiacal Animals series. Numbers in brackets refer to Chapters.

THE TORTOISE

Linked with: Snake

HISTORICAL BACKGROUND

The Chinese character for Tortoise shows the snakelike head above with claws on the left and shell on the right and the tail below (Figure 5.5).

The Tortoise (Figure 7.1) is considered the chief of the shelled animals. Its shell has the markings of the constellations of heaven and earth. The Tortoise has a snake head, dragon neck.

AUSPICIOUS MEANINGS OF TORTOISE

The Tortoise is one of the Four Spiritual Animals of China, along with the Phoenix, Dragon and Unicorn. In the Ganzhi System, it is the heraldic equivalent of the Black Snake of the North. It is sometimes called the Black Warrior, which is also the name of the Taoist deity of Wu-Tang Mountain (Eberhard, 1968, p.313).

The Tortoise is a symbol of longevity, strength and endurance. The Stork is said to live one thousand years but the Tortoise is said to live ten thousand years (Bowie, 1911, pp.86-96). Temples commonly keep pools of Tortoises and ponds of goldfish, the former to symbolize longevity and the latter wealth.

When the Carp has 300 scales it is in danger of being carried away by Dragons. Only the Tortoise could prevent this from happening. It must be placed with the Carp at least once a year. This could be the reason Fish ponds are found with Tortoise ponds in temples.

It is associated with Pan Ku, the fabled Creator of the universe and the world. The shell of the Tortoise represents the vault of heaven and its belly, the earth. The ancient Indians believed four Elephants stand on the shell of a great Tortoise to support the world. According to Chinese legends, the Goddess Nu Kua cut off the legs of the *Ao*, a great sea Tortoise, which use to support the world (Eberhard, 1968, p.406). *Ao* is also the fish-dragon on the roof which eats up fire and is also the name of the three mythical islands of the immortals of the southeast ocean.

Figure 7.1: The Tortoise – is a symbol of longevity, strength and endurance

From ancient times, the Chinese believed that the Tortoise shell could foretell the future and they thus form the ancient oracle shells. As far back as 2,300BC various regions of the empire were ordered to include as tributes Tortoise shells of at least a foot and two inches in length. It was then also a currency item. (Wu, 1982, p.6). Holes were bored through the shell which was then heated, causing the shell to crack. The lines of cracks from the holes would assume resemblance to various characters and were interpreted to form the oracle. Various markings were also made onto the shells. This is how we know certain Chinese words were of ancient origins – from these Tortoise oracle-shells.

YUAN AND THE THREE LEGGED PIEH AND YU

Among the turtles, there is reputed kind called *pieh*. *Pieh* is said to be a three legged *neng*. The character *pieh* is similar to that of *Pi* part of the named *Pi-Ling* who is the legendary emperor Great Yu (Eberhard, 1968, pp.199-200) as both of them performed similar feats. The character *Yu* means amphibious animal. The character *pieh* also equalled the hexagram *Li* in the I-Ching. This seems strange that *Li* should be connected with the water creatures, unless one connects *Li* to Yu's fire arrows which cause fever.

Yuan is another form of a turtle and is reputed to be evil. It drowns people and horses. It also rapes women. Women who bathe in rivers and are drowned are said to turn into turtles. This way, the urine of turtles is said to make a strong love charm. This evil animal appears connected to the Snake and the *chiao* dragon.

Yu is said to be a three-legged Tortoise and its "speckled dress" is an allusion to Pan-ku the fabled creator (Eberhard, 1968, p.193). This *Yu* is linked with the Bear as the lucky sign for a male child and is known as "short-fox" which concerns with immorality, singing in the fourth Moon and hence the frog, and related to the *fei* a grain parasite.

AUSPICIOUS LEGENDS ABOUT TORTOISE

Emperor Yu and the Ancient Tortoise Great Plan
According to legends, when Yu crossed the ocean, the Tortoise built a live bridge for him to cross (Eberhard, 1968, p.293).

The Tortoise is connected to Yu in another more important way. The mystic symbol of the Eight Diagrams or Pakua is a very common symbol in Chinese culture. The Hou-T'u system of the Pakua was believed to be brought to the first world emperor Fu-Hsi on the back of a Dragon-Horse (the Unicorn). But the Lo-Shu system of this Pakua is believed to be related to the ancient discovery of the Tortoise Great Plan by Emperor Yu. After some years as co-ruler with Shun, Yu succeeded Emperor Shun as emperor in 2205BC. When Yu was draining the Lo river into the Hwang-Ho, he uncovered a text called the Great Plan on the Tortoise which was supposed to contain the principles of the Tao. This Great Plan was consulted through a divination method known as the Tortoise and reeds.

Emperor Yu was said to mark the back of the Great Tortoise with nine numbers corresponding to the nine classifications to form the Lo-Shu arrangement of the Eight Diagrams or Pakua.

During the stirring times of the warring nations in the dying years of the Chou dynasty, the great Chinese sage Confucius or Kong Fu Tse, around 500BC, had compiled and edited a series of more ancient Chinese texts, besides expounding his own ideas, of which his Analects of Confucius is famous. Many of them were lost when in 220BC Emperor Shih Huang-Ti (builder of the Great Wall of China) of the short Chin dynasty ordered the Burning of Books in his persecution and massacres of the Chinese philosophers, particularly Confucians. But in 140BC, when Kung Wang, a prince of Lu, demolished a former building of Confucius, a broken wall revealed a hidden collection of books written in the ancient characters.

One of these books is the *Shu King* (q.v. Gorn, 1904) (another book is the I Ching which will have great significance in our discussions – the I Ching was one of the few books which escaped the great Burning of Books ordered by Emperor Shih Huang-Ti around 220BC). The original book is supposed to have one hundred sections, but only fifty-seven survived and form the basic of all modern texts of the *Shu King*. Although scholars have regarded certain sections as spurious (Creel, 1938), the *Shu King* is valuable as it contains the history of China from 2355BC to the end of the reign of Pin Wang in 719BC.

The Shang dynasty (1794 to 1120BC) was coming to an end. Emperor Chow Hsin, the last Shang emperor, was killed and Wu-Wang started the new Chou dynasty.

Within this *Shu King* is a remarkable record of how Emperor Wu-Wang, the founder of the Chou dynasty, consulted Ki-Tse, the former Minister of Instruction of the former Shang dynasty about how to govern his newly acquired nation. Ki-Tse (who, reputedly, was later to be allowed by the emperor to leave China to form the nation of Korea) told the emperor: "I have heard that in ancient days, Kwan, in trying to oppose the overwhelming waters, wrongly disposed of the five factors, and the Supreme Ruler was stirred with anger and did not communicate to him the Great Plan of the nine classifications; so that the invaluable principles were lost, and Kwan therefore was driven into exile. Yu was then appointed to succeed him, and Heaven conferred on Yu the Great Plan of the nine classifications and the invariable principles of right government were therefore regulated." (Gorn, 1904, p.160)

Emperor Wu-Wang was not unfamiliar with the aspects of the Great Plan because he had studied it before. The Emperor probably gained further insights through humbly seeking the advice of the ex-Minister Ki-Tse. This Great Plan composes of Five Factors (which are the five elements of water, fire, wood, metal and earth) and the Eight Regulators (the eight ministries in the government). The nine classifications propose how the Five Factors and Eight Regulators should be applied. The Emperor was urged to act in threefold consultation with the nobles, the people and the divination method of the Tortoise and reeds, with the status of planned actions determined as shown in the table below:

King Ruler	Nobles Government	People	Reeds	Tortoise	Status
+	+	+	+	+	Excellent
+	—	—	+	+	Fortunate
—	+	—	+	+	Good
—	—	+	+	+	Good
+	—	—	—	+	Internally good Externally bad

8

PAO HU, THE WHITE TIGER

Linked with: Bear, Unicorn, also Dog, Lion

The Tiger is the king of the beasts (Figure 8.1). The character *Wang* for king is supposedly being written all over his black-striped golden brown body. The Tiger is common in China and while the average would be about seven feet, some may be as long as twelve feet. Travel in northern China, where the Tiger abounds, could be dangerous.

The oracle bone script for Tiger is a picture of an animal with a long body, gaping jaws and prominent ears. The modern character for Tiger consists of the radical *hu* which represents the Tiger's stripes, while the *jen* signifies the supposed ability of the Tiger to stand on its hind legs like a man.

The Tiger was the principal animal god in ancient China. In Korea the Mountain God was a man riding the Tiger (Waterbury, 1952, p.8). The Tiger and the crestless bird appeared on Neolithic bronzes and also on the Shang An-Yang relics in China. Tiger images featured on ancient bronzes and its head is still reproduced in pairs on sides of bronzes often with a ring in its mouth. The *Shu King* mentions three men suggested for the Ministry of Forestry namely the Tiger, Bear and Grizzly Bear. It is the opinion of some that the Chinese *Lung* (alias Dragon) is the representative of lightning and, although serpentine, is derived from a composite Tiger (Waterbury, 1952, pp.80-82).

The various parts of the Tiger meat and bones have been attributed with all sorts of medicinal values in curing various diseases.

Figure 8.1: The Tiger and Chang Tao-Ling.
Tiger is a symbol of majesty, dignity and sternness. The figure of
Chang Tao-Ling and his Tiger is a popular paper charm against
evil. The Patriarch rides out on his Tiger on the 5th day of the 5th
moon, which is also the Dragon Boat Festival. Chang Tao-Ling's
8th ancestor was Taoist Chang Liang, the strategist who helped
Liu Pang to start the Han Dynasty.

HUNTING THE TIGER

The Tiger is a swift, powerful and ferocious animal which poses a constant threat to human life and his domestic livestock. It is a challenge to stalk and capture the Tiger. The reputation of being an elusive dangerous beast the Tiger makes its capture the highest achievement a hunter could accomplish. The Shang placed tiger hunting as a serious activity for a valiant hunter. Dangerous hunting has developed into a form of entertainment often depicted in dramas. Then it also evolved into a real sport combat between the beast and the man.

AUSPICIOUS MEANINGS OF TIGER

In spite of the threat the Tiger poses and that the Tiger has no special magical qualities, the Chinese respect the Tiger. Owing to its position as king of the wild animals, the Tiger is the natural symbol of majesty, dignity and sternness. The Tiger symbolizes courage and military prowess.

It is also the model of fierceness which all soldiers should imitate. Soldiers may wear Tiger skins and have Tigers images on their shields etc. to put on a fierce look to scare the enemies. Hence, the mighty fighter would be called Tiger-General.

The Tiger's sacred number is seven, which is a Yang number. Legend reputes it to live one thousand years where at five hundred it turns white and becomes the White Tiger. The White Tiger, Pao Hu, is the name given to the Western Quadrant of the Heavens. It is also the title conferred on the canonized Yin Cheng-Hsiu, a general of the last Yin Emperor and his image could be seen in Taoist temples (William, 1931, p.366).

If a grave site is located with the mountain at the rear and with a small hill in front, it is said to be sited with the green Dragon on the left (East) and the white Tiger on the right

(West) and the descendants would be wealthy and receive official greatness.

Should the White Tiger sit facing the door, if there is no misfortune there would be disaster. This saying is about the location of the front door. It is said that if the door is on the east side the *Lung* will bring a pearl, while the door at the west means that the Tiger waits to eat one up.

The Tiger is also an object of terror to demons. An image of the Tiger painted on walls and doors would scare the evil spirits away. His claws are powerful talismans and ashes prepared from his skin would be charm against sickness. The Tiger is also associated with the Taoist Pope Chang Tao-Ling, as well as Tsai Shen, the God of Wealth, described below.

However, a number of folktales reflect the Tiger's natural characteristics as a fierce but often dull-witted creature.

TAO-T'IEH OR BEAST OF GREED

The famous *Tao-T'ieh* or Beast of Greed designs which grace the designs of several Shang vessels and objects, are believed by some to be modelled on the fierce appearance of the Tiger (Hsu and Ward, 1984, p.49). The *Tao-T'ieh* or Beast of Greed is an embodiment warning against sensuality and avarice. It is represented by two enormous eyes and powerful mandibles with curved tusks. It was supposed to exist in Emperor Yao's times and was banished by Shun. It is found on bronze vessels. It is also depicted in relief on the inner wall of the "isolating shield wall" of main doors of official buildings to prevent evil spirits from entering the buildings. The image also serves as a warning against corruption to the officials going in and out of the buildings. Some swords also depict the *Tao-T'ieh* on the sword' hilts, ostentatiously to encourage purity and patriotism.

Although the *Tao-T'ieh* is a warning against avarice, it is at times confusingly used to denote the glutton and an ogre with a fat belly and thin face.

ASTROLOGICAL SIGNIFICANCE

The Feng-Shui declares that the universe is divided between and governed by four different beings, the Four Heraldic Animals, viz., the Azure Dragon on the East, the White Tiger on the West, the Red Phoenix on the South and Black Tortoise at the North (Figure 2.6, 3.1, Table 2.2).

The Tiger is thus the Animal of the West and was chosen to symbolize the western group of the Twenty-Eight Constellations during the warring states time (220BC). Later, when the West was represented by the colour white, the Tiger, too, became the White Tiger. The western position of the White Tiger is at times replaceable with the Bear or Unicorn (Hsu and Ward, 1984, pp.49, 467). As the *tiangan* symbol, the White Tiger has these significance:

Daring, power and passion. Terror against evil and eat ghosts and demons without pity. Its stripes denote auspicious mixture of Yang and Yin. Could be charged to protect young people against evil spirits. Ward off the three evils, viz. fire, thieves and ghosts.

The Tiger is also one of the Twenty-Eight Constellations ruled by the Heraldic Animal of the East, the Azure *Lung* (Table 2.3). The Tiger is the *Wei* constellation (means "Tail") and is linked with the element of Fire and the corresponding planet, Mars. It is an auspicious period falling on a Tuesday. The *Tong-Shu* says:

Blessings and numerous progeny would issue from building today. Descendants would have prosperity from business undertaken on this day. Marriages and funerals will bring imperial favour from the Capital.

Table 8.1

Zodiac Significance Of Tiger
Twelve Terrestrial Branches Significance

Order of Animals:	3rd
Hour ruled by Tiger:	3rd Hour, Yin (0300 to 0500)
Month	3rd Moon
Year	1914, 1926, 1938, 1950, 1962, 1974, 1986, 1998
Season	Early Spring
Direction	N60E
Western constellation	Aquarius
Ruling Planet	Uranus
Lucky Gemstone	Sapphire
Shade	Yang
Good points:	Courageous and optimistic. Dynamic, independent, with love of life. Born to command and not to obey, able to sway the crowd. Committed in doing things (no half measures). Sincere, honourable and humorous. Tolerant, humanistic, generous, capable of sacrifice especially in love as in romance. Good friend to have.
Bad points:	Rebellious, impulsive, unpredictable. Ill tempered, egoistic, prone to risks. Like grand tasks but do not check details. When desolate require encouraging words but not logic.
Dislike	criticism, Mean bully and vindictive
Others:	Sensual and romantic. Luck smiles if born between rising and setting of sun.
Compatible:	Boar, Dog, Horse, Rat, Sheep, Rooster.
Incompatible:	Chief adversary is Monkey. Others are Snake, Ox.
General Life:	Generally volatile Early years formative Old age often filled with regrets of things not done

The Tiger is the third of the twelve Zodiacal Animals or Terrestrial Branches (Figure 2.5). Its astrological characteristics are illustrated in Table 8.1. Despite there being no indications from the Zodiacal significance, it is considered unlucky for a woman to be born under the Tiger sign. Such a lady would "devour" her husband. She should be matched with another strong animal like the Tiger or Dragon.

AUSPICIOUS LEGENDS ABOUT TIGER

Guardian Spirit Of Agriculture

In very ancient times, the Tiger represents the harvest season. Peasants would pray to the Tiger for good harvests. The Tiger is regarded as the Guardian Spirit of Agriculture as it devours the drought demon, the *Han-pa*. Before irrigation was fully developed, the crops depended on the natural rains for water. The greatest danger to the crops would be inadequate rains during the growing season. So preventing the drought demon from sending down drought would guarantee a good harvest and this was why the Tiger was worshipped.

The Tiger, strange, considering its fierce quality, is also the Guardian Spirit of Children in later times. This could be because the fierce Tiger scares off the evil spirits. Or, it could be because parents would like their children to grow up to be as strong as the Tiger.

The Evil Tiger Spirit

The Tiger spirit is the chief of the animal spirits. The Tiger Spirit is Lin Chun who established the worship of his Tiger tribe – A fierce religion with human sacrifices and delighted in destruction and slaying. The proud and vicious Lin Chun is recognized as the ruler of animal demons. His paper charm, however, would give protection against evil as even the other evil spirits are afraid of him (Plopper, 1935, pp.104-105).

It is believed that the regular Tigers are all right, except a few which are regarded as were-Tigers which would hunt and eat men. Yet even this were-Tiger is supposed to harm only those whose sins of the present and previous lives required punishment. The were-Tiger eats those whom the gods command to be eaten. Heaven does not allow the were-Tiger to harm the good.

The evil Tiger spirit could turn into a human being, especially to a beautiful woman. It would get a man to marry it. It may even appear as a priest with the holy books and would quote sacred scriptures. He would then lead the dupe to a deserted place and kill and devour him. This Tiger, however, would see his own form in the mirror and would take fright at its own fierce image and flees. Those who know would carry a mirror with them and test all newcomers. Those eaten by Tigers would become demons known as *ch'ang kuei* and would be the Tiger's servants. These servants would ensnare others into the Tiger's traps so as to be able to free themselves to continue their journey into the Underworld. Otherwise, they would be trapped to roam as restless spirits on earth. The were-Wolf is as dangerous and feared but not as common as the were-Tiger. The Chinese would hunt, trap and kill the Tigers and Wolves.

One of the Eighteen *Lohans* or priests-monk is known as the Repressor of Tigers and may be seen drawn with a Tiger over his shoulders (Plopper, 1935, pp.155-156).

CHANG TAO-LING RIDING THE TIGER

The Tiger is the beast on which Chang Tao-Ling, the Taoist Pope, rides (Figure 8.1). The legend of Chang Tao-ling is as follows (Plopper, 1935, pp.210-212): Chang Tao-Ling was the eighth descendant of the Taoist immortal Chang Liang who lived in 200BC and was the Councillor of the first Emperor of the Han dynasty. Having placed the emperor on the throne Chang Liang had retired from the world to seek the elixir of life. Chang Tao-Ling was born in AD34 in Hangchow, Chekiang at T'ien Mu-Shan. He later lived in Lung Hu Shan (Dragon-Tiger Mountain) in Kiangsi where his representative still lives. He lived for 123 years when he took the elixir of life and joined the Immortals. He was supposed to have the power to demote the City God and appoint officials of the Underworld. His priests use his name on charms to frighten the demons. He is particularly worshipped on the fifth day of the fifth month when he was supposed to ride out on a Tiger with the cup of immortality in his left hand and his sword in the right hand to destroy demons and protect the people. The Tiger would grasp his magic seal with one paw and with the other paw tramples down the Five Poisonous Animals. Pictures of him with accessories would be put up the fifth day of the fifth month to ward off evil influences of calamity and sickness. The Artemesia could also be used instead of the sword.

TSAI SHEN RIDING THE TIGER

Even as the Tiger is ridden by Chang Tao-Ling, the Tiger is also associated with Hsuan T'an, the Tsai Shen God of Wealth, chief of the five gods of affluence, holding a silver ingot in one hand and riding the Tiger, or the Tiger would be by his side. Or he may be represented as the Tiger itself. These five brothers would go for a walk on the fifth day of the first month. For this reason, on the fifth day of the Lunar New Year every door would be open to welcome him. Sometimes, Tsai Shen himself would be represented as a Tiger and this is the basis of the several Tiger gods found in some parts of China.

THE GODDESS HSI WANG-MU

Many fairy tales tell of Hsi Wang-Mu, the famous Queen Mother of the West. She has a Leopard's tail, Tiger head and teeth, tangled hair which shines on her white head. She has a stone city with a golden house and a cave in which she lives. The stone chamber was north of the Lake of Immortals and the Salt Pond. Three green birds fetch her food. Like the Tiger, Hsi Wang-Mu is always associated with mountains and the west. She was said to achieve the Tao, but no one really knows her beginning and her end. She administers Heaven's calamities on five types of crimes.

Hsi Wang-Mu dwelled in a large cave in the Kun-Lun mountains. The Kun-Lun mountains are about 2,700 miles west of China and lie to the south of the western sea. They lie on the shores of the Shifting Sands, back of the Red River and in front of the Black River – these descriptions if true would place the actual geographical location of the Kun-Lun mountains in the Middle East! Legends claim they were inhabited by a deity with the face of a human being, body of a Tiger, and with stripes and a tail both of which are white ... said to be in Kun-Lun mountains wearing a high hair comb with Tiger's teeth, a leopard's tail, living in a cave and called Hsi Wang-Mu.

The White Tiger is therefore also the symbol of Hsi Wang-Mu and not unnaturally the animal is the symbol of the West in the Four Heraldic Animals.

Table 8.2

Tiger's Sayings

The Tiger is associated with sayings about great men and honourable things:

- Dragon step and Tiger gaze. Meaning: Awesome aura.
- Walking like Dragon and pacing like Tiger. Meaning: Dignified bearing.
- The dead person leaves his reputation as a Tiger his skin: Everyone leaves a reputation.
- Tiger does not mix with deer: People of contrary traits should not come together.

However, strong as a Tiger is, even a Tiger must await the right time and condition to do things:

- The Tiger brings wind and the Dragon clouds. Meaning: Everything has its natural following which do not happen by chance.
- Dragon returns to the water and the Tiger to the mountain. Meaning: Going back to one's own element and environment where one's talents could be used fully.
- The Tiger cannot resist all the dogs: Even the powerful cannot resist everybody.
- Even a Tiger must take a nap: One blunders at times.
- Evil characteristics are commonly associated with Tigers and snakes. Many Tiger sayings reflect the evil and treacherous nature of the animal:
- Laughing face Tiger. Meaning: He is smiling but plotting to kill you.
- A paper Tiger: A threatening front but no real power (also: To prick a hole in a paper Tiger – to show him up).
- Tiger which does not eat man is still evil outside: His evil reputation continues even after the evil person changed.

THE UNICORN – KI LI

Linked with: Tiger, Bear also Dog, Lion

HISTORICAL BACKGROUND

The Unicorn is one of the mythological animals (Figure 9.1) and is considered as the prince of all beasts, just as the Phoenix is the emperor of all birds and the *Lung* the chief of the reptilian animals.

It is one of the Four Spiritual or Intelligent Animals and it is supposed to be able to appear and disappear at will and its appearance brings happiness and good fortune and is blessings to those who see it. However, it is not shown in the Four Supernatural Animals of the Chinese *Feng-Shui*, its position apparently being taken up by the White Tiger on the West. According to Hsu and Ward (1984) the Unicorn, the Tiger and the Bear are inter-equivalent.

The Chinese Unicorn or *Ling* or *ki li* has a colourful stag body, horse hoofs, ox tail, wolf forehead, parti-coloured skin with a single horn with a fleshy tip from the forehead of the male. Sometimes there are two horns – the female has no horn. The male is *ch'i* and the female is *li* – hence the combined name *ki li*. Another description is that it is a benevolent animal with an antelope's body, ox tail and a single horn which is flesh-tipped showing its harmless nature. Its skin is of five colours of the Empire, red, yellow, blue, white and black. It is yellow beneath. It is twelve cubits high and walks on water as well as on land. It never eats nor drinks dirty things. Like the Phoenix, it also emits a highly musical voice.

It is a solitary creature. Like the solitary Phoenix it never hurts other creatures nor thread unnecessarily on living things.

The *ki li* is drawn in art surrounded by fire or clouds. The Goddess of Fecundity holding a child in her arms rides on a Unicorn. Where the dragon is embroidered onto Imperial clothes, the Unicorn is placed onto clothes of military officers of first ranks. The Taoist Immortal T'ung-t'ien Chiao-chu, first of the Patriarchs and one of the most powerful of the sect, wore a red robe embroidered with white Cranes and he rides a *k'uei niu*, a kind of buffalo-Unicorn, who would stamp the enemies of the Taoist (Werner, 1922, p.133).

Figure 9.1: The Unicorn.
The Unicorn is the symbol of perfect goodness,
longevity, grandeur, filial piety, illustrious descendants and wise
administration. The Unicorn appeared to Confucius's mother at
his birth and Confucius died soon after a Unicorn was killed.

UNICORN'S PRECIPICE

In the legendary Kun-Lun Mountain the western home of the Chinese gods is called the Unicorn Precipice where the scenery is enchanting and beautiful with all sorts of colours of flowers, trees, animals, birds and buildings. The Unicorn Precipice is like the Garden of Eden, a serene place where the mild Unicorn would roam in (Werner, 1922, p.154). The Kun-Lun Mountain is known in Chinese culture to be in the far West. It is also the fabled place where the first two human beings, Fu-Hsi and his sister Nu Kua, were created. Hence, the Unicorn's Precipice is very likely the Chinese memory of the Biblical Garden of Eden.

AUSPICIOUS MEANINGS OF UNICORN

The Unicorn is the symbol of perfect goodness, longevity, grandeur, filial piety, illustrious descendants and wise administration. It is a creature of goodwill, gentleness to every living thing and has all the good qualities of hairy animals. The saying is:

> May the Unicorn's hoof give you luck.

The Unicorn symbolizes purity and also the solitude and monastic life. It was so in ancient Egypt and Persia and also in Christianity. In the west, the Unicorn is naturally a fierce animal but is instantly subdued to gentleness by a virgin. Some western murals depicted the Unicorn on a young lady's lap with a man spearing its side – the Unicorn represents Christ, the lady Mary. It is a very common heraldic emblem, often used in substitute to the Dragon (Whittick, 1960, pp.285-286).

When a saying such as "There is the *Ki li* among quadrupeds", it means that there is a superior man in the group. It is the herald of good government. The wisdom of the Unicorn enables it to detect the appearance of wise kings and sages.

Hence, when the Unicorn appears it means a sage is born. It appears only when there is benevolent rule in the realm. It appeared during the times of Yao and Shun (Williams, 1931, p.382) and also Yu and Tang (Plopper, 1935, p.114). Thus when a Unicorn appeared and was unfortunately killed in a ducal hunt in 481BC, Confucius lamented over its death and laid down his pen, wrote no more and died a few years later (Wu, 1982, p.6). This was also the last reputed appearance of the Unicorn. Thus, some writers believe the Unicorn was some form of quadruped now extinct.

There is a saying: The Tiger and the Leopard are always anxious lest they meet the Unicorn. That is, no matter how powerful is, he would meet someone else of whom he would be afraid of.

THE UNICORN AND CONFUCIUS

Unlike the fierce western Unicorn contending with the Lion for the heraldic crown, the Chinese Unicorn is essentially a mild beast, preferring the company of scholars rather than warrior knights.

Confucius' mother was childless for a long time and she yearned for a child. She became pregnant when she stepped over the footprints of the Unicorn when she was on her way to Mount Ni to pray for a child (Williams, 1931, p.383).

According to legend, a Unicorn appeared to Confucius' mother before he was born. The creature presented her with a jade tablet inscribed with "the son of the essence of water will follow the fallen house of Chou and become a throneless king" (Plopper, 1935, p.114). Hence, Confucius' greatness and his futile career in trying to change kingdoms for the better were foretold.

It was said that when Confucius was born the Phoenix appeared, the Unicorn was playing in the background with

Confucius' mother watching. So, the Unicorn is also the symbol for children and the charm says:

> Unicorn bringing sons.
> Desiring the Unicorn's foot.

Another appeared shortly before Confucius' death when he was writing the Ch'un Ch'iu. While Shu Sun Shi was gathering firewood he caught a Unicorn and accidentally broke one of its legs. Confucius recognized the wounded Unicorn which died. Confucius threw his pen away and stopped writing believing that his doctrines would not gain way from the omen of the death of the Unicorn. His disciples finished the book. (Plopper, 1935, p.114)

THE UNICORN
AND WORLD FIRST EMPEROR FU-HSI

The Unicorn is also associated with the birth of the Chinese language and writing.

Long ago, it appeared as the Dragon-Horse to the first world Emperor Fu-Hsi with the mystic map Hou-T'u on its back. This Hou-T'u is an arrangement of the nine numbers in a cross pattern and is reputed to be the basis of origin of the Chinese language. The Unicorn is thus associated with sacred writings and wise good men who could appreciate the sacred writings.

In a similar version, the Buddhists represent this animal as carrying the Book of the Law on its back. This seems to be a modification of the *Journey to the West* tale of the Dragon-Horse which was the steed of the monk who, accompanied by the famous Monkey God, went west to bring back the Buddhist scriptures.

THE BEAR

Linked with: Tiger, Unicorn

INTRODUCTION

The Bear is quite common in China. There is the Black Bear, *Ursus tibetanus* and *U. ussurious* and the famous Panda Bear, *Aeluropus melanoleucus*. The Bear's paw is considered a food delicacy. It lives in the mountains and hibernates. It is said that people of the first three dynasties of ancient China made sacrifice to the Bear. It is also said that the male consort of Hsi Wang-Mu resided in the East and wore a black Bear on his head (Eberhard, 1968, p.470).

AUSPICIOUS MEANINGS OF BEAR

It is the Chinese symbol of bravery and strength. It is also considered a lucky animal, being a sign preceding the coming of a male child. If one sees a Bear in a dream, it means you are going to have a male child. A Bear pillow is auspicious for producing sons. (Eberhard, 1968, pp.193,469).

The Panda was formerly embroidered on robes of officials of the sixth rank.

The Bear is sacred to Artemis, Greek Goddess of War, to whom it may be sacrificed. The Bear is regarded as a heavy, rough creature and typifies a rough, uncouth, bad-tempered person not unmixed with affection owing to a natural liking for the cub (Whittick, 1960, pp.150-151).

ASTROLOGICAL SIGNIFICANCE OF BEAR

There is also an ancient link between the Bear and the Chinese Ganzhi system of astrology. Chou Li described a Bear Dance (Waterbury, 1952, pp.11-12). An official called the "Inspector of the Region or Universal Preserver" would impersonate a Bear entering houses to drive away demons and diseases. This Bear, the Fang-Siang-Che, would be accompanied by twelve persons disguised as various animals and birds. The twelve animals were said to represent the summoning of the animal spirits of the various localities. This Fang-Siang-Che ceremony is also known as the great *No* Festival carried out in the twelfth month to exorcise evil (Eberhard, 1972, p.6).

Hence, the Bear is the Chinese representation of the polar system of *Ursa Major* (Figure 10.1). Thus, the Fang-Siang-Che ceremony revolving around the Bear and the twelve animals was really an invocation of the full Ganzhi System, namely, the *tiangan* Ten Celestial Stems represented by the Bear and the *dizhi* Twelve Terrestrial Branches represented by the Twelve Zodiac Animals.

The Great Yu is said to have performed a shamanistic dance disguised as a Bear and he was said to be interrupted in his dance by his wife. Bear meat is taboo for these priests and in the sacrifices to temples raised for Yu. In this connection, the Bear is said to be a form of a large river-pig (Eberhard, 1968, pp.259,353).

In fact, the Bear shares with the Pig as being the animal of the thirteenth constellation (q.v. Pig).

The Bear or Fang-Siang-Che Dance and the Dance or Steps of Yu are the same dance. This dance is also performed to kill the Serpent by birds such as the Stork, Dove (q.v.). In Taoist magic to combat black magic, the Dance of Yu is invoked against Mao Shan Serpent magic.

Thus, Emperor Ta Yu, founder of the Hsia dynasty, is linked to the Bear. Ta Yu is also linked with the Monkey (q.v.). There are probably some very significant auspiciousness of the Bear to the Chinese in very ancient times but this information has been lost through time.

Figure 10.1: The Bear.
Symbol of strength and bravery. The Bear was the central animal in the ill-known ancient Chinese Fang-Siang-Che ceremony which appears to be the equivalent of the significance of Ursa Major (Great Bear).

THE TWELVE ZODIACAL ANIMALS

INTRODUCTION

The Twelve Terrestrial Branches of the Ganzhi System denote the twelve units of direction and time: Twelve Terrestrial Branches (*Dizhi*) also known as Twelve Earthly Branches or Duodenary series:

1.	Zi (rat)	7.	Wu (horse)
2.	Chou (ox)	8.	Wei (sheep)
3.	Yin (tiger)	9.	Shen (monkey)
4.	Mao (horse)	10.	You (cock)
5.	Chen (dragon)	11.	Xu (dog)
6.	Si (serpent)	12.	Hai (pig)

The Terrestrial Branches apply to factors on the Earth plane. The units of the *dizhi* system are best known for their association with the Twelve Zodiacal Animals (Figure 2.5), covering the twelve years of a Jupiter cycle.

Besides their popular association with the Twelve Zodiacal Animals, these Twelve Terrestrial Branches are also associated with the twelve double hours of the day, the twelve months of the year and also the twelve compass points (Figure 2.4). They also mark the twelve Terrestrial directions and the location of the earth dragon *ch'i* forces.

The association of the twelve years with the twelve animals arose from a belief that the different years come under different animal spirits' influences which could be reflected by the behaviour of the corresponding animals. That is, the characteristics of these animals symbolize the nature of the different years.

ORIGINS OF THE TWELVE TERRESTRIAL BRANCHES

According to Tun Li-Ch'en, AD1000 (Derk, 1965, p.110), the Twelve Zodiacal Animals are generally supposed to be of Turkish origin, though this has not been conclusively proven. Needham (1959, p.405) also notes several authorities which maintain that the Chinese took the Twelve Zodiacal Animals from neighbouring Turks or from the ancient Middle East. The naming of years after animals continues in numerous Asians cultures.

Although the Twelve Terrestrial Branches of the animals are said not to be defined until the fifth century BC, the twenty-two symbols of the Ganzhi System were already being used during the Hsia dynasty (Ho, 1975, p.240). Hence, the Twelve Terrestrial Branches must also be as old.

In fact, Needham (1959, p.398) points out that the Old Babylonian (circa 3,000BC) divided time into twelve equal double hours. The Twelve Zodiacal Animals system is not only very old but it is more than likely that it derived from the older Old Babylonian system.

The Twelve Zodiacal Animals are among the animals of the Twenty-Eight Constellations. The Twenty-Eight Constellations may therefore be the origin of the Zodiacal Animals.

THE FANG-SIANG-CHE CEREMONY

The Zodiacal Animals could also be linked with the Bear Dance of Chou Li (Waterbury, 1952, pp.11-12). An official called the "Inspector of the Region or Universal Preserver" would impersonate a Bear by wearing a bear costume and went into houses to drive away demons and diseases. This Fang-Siang-Che, accompanied by twelve persons disguised as various animals and birds, was also invoked during the Han dynasty to drive away great calamity. The twelve animals were said to represent the summoning of the animal spirits of the various localities. A ram and a cock would normally be sacrificed at the gate.

The Fang-Siang-Che ceremony is also known as the *No* Festival. During the twelfth month, there would be a great *No* Festival carried out to exorcize evil. A great procession would be held to display the twelve "animals" – the rat, cow, tiger, hare, dragon, serpent, horse, sheep, monkey, cock, dog and pig. They would marched through the town under the direction of a sorcerer who was dressed as a bear (Eberhard, 1972, p.6).

The Bear could be the Chinese polar system of *Ursa Major* along with the North Pole Star and other polar stars. Thus, the Fang-Siang-Che ceremony was really an invocation of the full Ganzhi System namely, the *tiangan* Ten Celestial Stems represented by the Bear and the *dizhi* Twelve Terrestrial Branches represented by the twelve animals (Figure 2.4).

The Fang-Siang-Che ceremony would only be performed during times of great calamities which were caused by irregularities along both the Heavenly and Earthly fields. The priest would summon the forces of both Heaven and Earth, as represented by the two different groups of animals.

This ancient Bear Dance seems similar to other animal dances in other cultures.

GENERAL AUSPICIOUS SIGNIFICANCE OF ZODIACAL ANIMALS

While each of the Twelve Zodiacal Animals has its special auspicious significance within the Terrestrial Branches system, they also have interlinked significance in other sets of symbolism (other than the Twenty-Eight Constellations).

New Year Period

The days of the New Year period could be dedicated to the birthdays of various animals and even crops as follows (Burkhardt, 1982, p.10):

1st Day	Fowl and chickens
2nd Day	Dogs
3rd Day	Pigs
4th Day	Ducks (not a zodiac animal)
5th Day	Cattle
6th Day	Horses
7th Day	Human beings (not a zodiac animal)
8th Day	Rice and cereals
9th Day	Fruits and vegetables
10th Day	Corn and barley

If that day is fine with absence of wind or rains, then the forthcoming year would be good for the said beast or crop.

The Pakua Eight Diagrams

Each of the Eight Diagrams is also associated with an animal as follows (Burkhardt, 1982, p.212):

Trigram Image		Direction King Wen	Fu-Hsi	Animal	Direction Zodiac	Heraldic
Ch'ien	Heaven	NW	S	Horse	S*	
Tui	Lake	W	SE	Sheep	S-SW	E
Li	Fire	S	E	Pheasant		S*
Chen	Thunder	E	NE	LUNG	E-SE	E*,C
K'un	Earth	SW	N	Ox	N-NE	C
Ken	Mountain	NE	NW	Dog	W-NW	W
Kan	Water	N	W	Pig	N-NW	N*
Sun	Wind	SE	SW	Fowl	W S	

There are only some weak similarities of the association of each of the Eight Diagrams with an animal to the natural positions of the Twelve Zodiacal Animals and the Four Heraldic Animals along the compass points. The basis of this association of the Eight Diagrams is obscured and may represent a variant of the traditional association of the Terrestrial Branches with the compass directions.

Marriage Pairs

The Chinese Almanac, *Tong-Shu*, advises against certain pairs of animals undertaking a marriage agreement (Wong, 1967, p.39; Burkhardt, 1982, p.81):

> The white horse cannot share a stall with the black cow.
>
> The boar and the monkey quickly parted.
>
> The sheep and the rat quickly separate.
>
> The dragon flies to the clouds at the sight of the hare.
>
> The golden cock sheds tears at the sight of the dog.
>
> If the snake catches a glimpse of the tiger, it is like being wounded with a knife.

The *Tong-Shu* also provides a list of these favoured pairs of animals: Rat-Ox, Tiger-Pig, Dog-Hare, Cock-*Lung*, Sheep-Horse and Monkey-Snake.

It should be borne in mind that the unsuitable or favoured pair combinations could also be affected by the elements. In fact, there is incompatibility between animals of the Twelve Zodiacal Animals set due to that they often have common element signs in the Twenty-Eight Constellations system (q.v.). This gives rise to speculations that the Twelve Zodiacal Animals are really derived from the animals of the Twenty-Eight Constellations.

12

THE RAT

HISTORICAL BACKGROUND

The Rat is a common animal and a notorious pest in the house as well as among the crops in the land (Figure 12.1). These animals are numerous. Sounds of nibbling during the funeral times could be caused by Rats and mice eating the unattended food.

The Cat is, of course, the natural enemy of the Rat. The ancient Chinese character for Cat is that of an animal catching Rats in the rice field. The Cat is known for catching the Rats which come to get the grains. As Rats destroy silkworm and Cats keep Rats away, the Cats are also regarded as protectors of the Silkworms.

The Chinese character for Rat shows its ancient pictogram with head, whiskers, feet and tail.

The Rat is a recognized item of food in China but had been a carrier of bubonic plague in China. Its meat is supposed to be good for those bald people who want to have their hair grow back.

The ancient Chinese believed that the Rat could turn into a quail and the quail into a Rat during the eighth Moon (Williams, 1931, p.304)

The Rat is a Yin animal reputed to be able to live up to 300 years. When it is 100 years old it would turn white. The White Rat is able to divine the person's luck for a whole year and predict happenings 1,000 miles away. When tyrants rule and the people are oppressed, the White Rat will emerge (Wong, 1967, p.29).

Figure 12.1: The Rat.
Symbol of timidness and meanness, but also of craftiness. The first
animal of the Twelve Zodiac Animals, it is said to have betrayed
the Cat, which was left out of the Zodiac.

AUSPICIOUS MEANINGS OF RAT

It is the emblem of timidity and meanness, though also of sharp intelligence. It is a symbol of wealth obtained by diligence.

Li Szu, the famous Legalist, once saw Rats eating away at the corn in a corner of the granary without fear of man or dog. He declared: "Man's perspicacity is incomparable to that of the Rat." (Wong, 1967, p.30).

The Rat could also be considered loyal. This is based on a tale that a Rat continued to harass a Snake which had eaten another Rat (Wong, 1967, p.30).

The nineteenth Day of the 1st Moon is the Rats Wedding Day (some put it as the tenth day). It is celebrated to induce the King of rodents to divert the depredations of his subjects to those less mindful of their religious obligations. It is believed that the Rat is immortal and spit out its intestines on the last day of each month, rendering it newly born (Eberhard, 1968, p.336).

Should a large Rat with a large stomach paunch enters the house it should not be chased out but treated as an honoured guest. For such a Rat is the Money Rat whose arrival is an omen of approaching wealth. The Rat is not the only money-spinner, others such as a red spider, a form of northern centipede and even the snake is classified under the same category (Burkhardt, 1982, pp.197-198).

Lu Hsiung who became a military official attributed his success to the auspiciousness of a brood of five Rats staying in the oven of his house. (Wong, 1967, p.30)

There is a story of Chang Hsien, guardian of children, shooting at the Rat with a bow without arrow. There were five children clinging to his red robes and there might be a group of two-tailed Cats. The Rat shot at is a red winged black Rat on a cloud. Here, the Rat is the emblem of wealth and its acquisition is supposed to be an endowment for the family clinging to his clothings. Chang Hsien is said to be identified with Chang Kuo, the Immortal who loves sport and is connected with marital happiness and birth of children. The number "five" of the children is a "Five Fortunes" number and the image of Chang Hsien with the five children would be a powerful talisman for family blessings.

Rat is one of the five feared household animals which could cause disturbances due to insanity. The saying is "Like running against the claws of the five animals". The five animals are the Fox, Weasel (or Polecat), Hedgehog, Snake and Rat which are feared and worshipped as the Five Great Families. Their particular habit of lying down on the way often cause people to step on their "claws" and thus were attacked. (Plopper, 1935, pp.103-104; Eberhard, 1968, p.314)

The coming of a strange Cat to the household is an omen of approaching poverty. It is supposed to foresee where it will find plenty of Rats and mice in consequence of approaching dilapidation, following the ruin or poverty of its inhabitants. It is also considered very unlucky when a Cat is stolen from a house.

MEASURES AGAINST THE RAT

As the Rat is generally regarded as a threat, various measures would be devised against the rodent.

During the Budding Moon or 2nd Moon, women would worship the White Tiger on the sixth of March. Paper images of the White Tiger would be carried around to keep off Rats and snakes and prevent quarrels. Imperial sacrifices used to be offered to the sun for promoting the agricultural growth while the people propitiated the farm gods. It is natural that two things would be important; rains and safety of crops from pests, of which the Rat is one. Hence, the practice of using the big cat, the Tiger to scare off the Rats.

THE GANZHI POSITION OF THE RAT
TIANGAN POSITION OF RAT

The Rat is not one of the Four Heraldic Supernatural Animals. However, it is the eleventh constellation *Hsu* (the "Void"), which belongs to the Northern Quadrant of the Black Tortoise-Snake. (Table 2.3). It is associated with the sun and falling on a Sunday which is an inauspicious time. the *Tong-Shu* says:

> Building today is disastrous. Children will sleep undesirably. Debauchery will sweep through the family from a lack of rites. Wives, sons and grandsons will sleep in other beds.

DIZHI POSITION OF RAT

The Rat is the first of the twelve Zodiacal Animals or Terrestrial Branches (Figure 2.5). Its astrological characteristics are illustrated in Table 12.1 and 12.2.

The *Tong Shu* provides this saying about the marriage of the Rat which preclude a happy union:

> The sheep and Rat quickly separate.

Marital contracts between a person born under the sign of the Rat and another under the sign of the sheep would be short-lived. In the Malaysian context, matrimony between the Rat and the Dog would also be disastrous as the Dog would attack the Rat (Wong, 1967, p.41).

AUSPICIOUS LEGENDS ABOUT RAT

The Guardian of the North, Mo Li-Shou, wields two whips and carried a panther-skin sack containing a creature known as Hua Hu Tiao. In the sack it resembles a white Rat, but at large it takes the form of a winged white elephant of carnivorous habit. (Burkhardt, 1982, p.183). According to

legend, the Mountain God, Erh Lang or Yang Chien killed
Mo Li-Shou and obtained this magic Rat as his new pet.

Table 12.1

The Zodiacal Significance Of Rat

Terrestrial Branches Significance

Order of Animals:	1st
Hour ruled by Rat	1st Hour, Tzu (2300 to 0100)
Month	1st moon
Year	1912, 1924, 1936, 1948, 1960, 1972, 1984, 1996
Season	Winter
Direction	North
Western constellation	Sagittarius
Ruling Planet	Jupiter
Lucky Gemstone	Carbuncle
Shade	Yin
Symbol:	Wealth and prosperity
Good points:	Lively, sociable charming, easy to get along. Hard working, thrifty. Able to sense danger. Irritable but can control himself. Critical intellectual and therefore also symbol of intelligence. Honest and meticulous. Good adviser but not of oneself – therefore lucky and generous to friends. Devote in love even if not loved back
Bad points:	Uncommunicative, secretive, Self-seeking, greedy, self-indulging. Love to criticize and gossip. Can be nasty due to extreme aggressiveness and pettiness. Overambitious Make abusive use of friends
Others:	Sentimental Better life if born at night and summer and can control his greed – this is the bold daring Rat Rat born in the day – timid and afraid in life.
Best occupations:	Writers, historians
Compatible:	Ox
Incompatible:	Worst adversary is Horse
Others:	Cock, Sheep

HOW THE ZODIAC WAS NAMED

To make it easier to remember the years of the Sexagenary Cycle, the Immortals announced their intention to name the years after twelve animals. The first twelve animals who reached the place at a particular time would represent the twelve years.

When they were about to announce that the Ox who arrived first thus its name for first year, a squeaking sound protested. The Immortals saw on the head of the Ox was the small Rat who jumped off to claim its right for the first year. The Rat had unknowingly taken a ride on the Ox and thus was able to arrive at the place together with the Ox.

The Ox protested at the trick. But the Immortals could not decide as both animals were the first to arrive. The furious Ox ridiculed the Rat: "You are too tiny and insignificant for the honour."

The Rat retorted: "You are a boaster. Let us parade before the judges and see who is really so big." So a contest was held to further decide who the first year should be named after.

The two animals paraded before the judges. The Rat blew itself to twice its normal size. The judges had not seen such a large Rat and the abnormal size attracted the judges' attention. "See how large a giant the Rat is! This gigantic Rat is really incomparable."

When the Ox heard all the exclamations about the Rat it decided to resign from the contest. So the first year was named after the Rat.

THE CAT WHO MISSED THE ZODIAC ROLL

The Rat and the Cat were once the best of friends. One day, Buddha called up the animals to decide how the lunar years be named. It was agreed that the first twelve animals who finished the race would have the honour of the years being named after them. So the Cat and Rat who were then best friends made a pact to wake one another up. They slept on the same bed on the eve of the meeting with the Buddha.

Table 12.2

Effects Of Tiangan Factor on Zodiac Significance Of Rat

The *tiangan* factor would predispose the Rat along the following trends:

Metal	Idealistic, intensively emotional Wise in investment Show-off Athletic Easily moved to jealousy
Water	A thinking Rat Will be respected Shrewd Too outspoken
Wood	Success orientated Amiable Farsighted Loves security and worry about the future Good talker
Fire	Chivalrous, dynamic, idealistic and ambitious Generous Independent and not so well-disciplined Lack diplomacy
Earth	Realistic, but can be over-practical and stingy Thorough in work Self-righteous and intolerant Never takes chances Fortune slow but sure

The Rat woke up early in the morning and rushed off. It managed to stealthily thumb a lift from the humble Ox and won the race after some further contest.

In the meantime the Cat woke up and found the Rat missing and realized he had been betrayed. The Cat rushed off to the race but was too late. The naming of the lunar year after first twelve animals were done. Since then the Cat could never forgive the Rat and always seek an opportunity to hunt and kill the Rat.

Another legend puts it that invitations were sent to twelve animals including the Cat (Kwok, 1989, pp.40-41). The Rat then tricked the Cat who did not arrive when the naming was done. The divine adviser sent a servant to fetch another animal. The first animal he saw was the Pig.

13

THE OX

Link with: Domestic equivalent of Golden *Lung*

HISTORICAL BACKGROUND

The cattle, along with the Pig, are sold for food. However, in deference to the role of the Water-Buffalo in working the land, the Chinese may avoid eating beef. Avoidance of beef eating may also be later influenced by Indian Buddhism faith where beef eating is frowned on. But Eberhard (1968) notes that the ancient Chinese has a cattle cult before Indian influence came into China.

The bones of the Ox, Horse and Sheep were seldom found in archaeological digs in China until after around 1400BC. This indicates the animal was an introduction from the West, albeit in quite ancient times.

Shen Nung, the Chinese World Third Emperor and God of Agriculture, is said to have a bovine head (Eberhard, 1968, p.228). The Bull horns formed the head-dress of ancient kings in Assyria and Babylon. There are reasons to believe that the Tartars took this headdress as they were descendants of the Middle East nations.

AUSPICIOUS MEANINGS OF OX

Ox is the emblem of spring and agriculture. In the Chinese Almanac, the *Tong-Shu*, the characteristics of the Spring Ox and its cowherd (Figure 13.1) would foretell the climatic nature of the coming year.

Beef eating in the Chinese *Materia Medica* is attributed with great strengthening, possibly owing to the muscular unwieldy beast.

There is an ancient festival called the "meeting of spring" which is a farmers' holiday. There would be a ceremonial ploughing of the land and beating and sacrifice of the Spring Ox. The ceremony is similar to the procession of the Bull Apis in ancient Egypt (Williams, 1931, pp.265-266; Burkhardt, 1982, p.11). According to legend, this ceremony was performed by the founder of the Chou Dynasty when the Shang was finally defeated around 1122BC. He could not proceed more than 900 odd steps upon which his adviser Chiang Tzu-ya foretold that the Chou Dynasty would last some 900 years – which it did, the longest reigning Chinese dynasty.

Figure 13.1: The Divine Cowherd and the Ox.
The Ox is the symbol of spring and agriculture. It is also an ancient symbol of power, fertility and strength.

Table 13.1

The Zodiacal Significance Of Ox
Terrestrial Branches Significance

Order of Animals:	2nd
Time ruled by Ox	2nd Hour, Ch'ou (0100-0300)
Month	2nd moon
Year	1901, 1913, 1925, 1937, 1949, 1961, 1973, 1985
Season	End of Winter
Direction	N30E
Western constellation	Capricorn
Ruling Planet	Saturn
Lucky Gemstone	White Onyx
Shade	Yin
Symbol:	Enduring Prosperity through hard work
Good points:	Reliable, sincere, cool, patient and meticulous. a tireless dedicated obedient conventional worker. Neat, unpretentious and modest. Fond of solitude, has few friends who are however very faithful to him. Hidden resolute logical fair mind, good listener. Systematic in a conventional way – likes tradition. Do things to last.
Bad points:	Stubborn – difficult to change views. Can be carried away with convention – can be too rigid. Not generous with money. Naive about love and often too fussy. Bear grudges for long time.
Others:	Happy youth but would eventually realize the responsibilities of adult age. No free ride in life but will emerge winners through own efforts
Compatible	Cockerel, Rat, Snake
Incompatible	Dog, Sheep, Tiger

Table 13.2

Effects Of Tiangan Factor on Zodiac Significance Of Ox

The "tiangan" factor would predispose the Ox along the following trends:

Metal	Strong will and often clash with people
	Tough and arrogant
	Narrow-minded and vengeful
	Lot of stamina
	Not affectionate
Water	Realistic Ox
	Calm, patient and determined
	More reasonable and flexible
	Work well with others
Wood	Less rigid and considerate
	Socially graceful
	Respected for integrity and ethics
	Innovative and progressive
	Great heights of wealth and fame
Fire	Combustible performer
	Drawn to power and ambition
	Forceful and proud (but not as much as Metal Ox)
	Materialistic with superiority complex
	Hard working
	Honest and fair
Earth	Enduring but less creative
	Practical and industrious
	Not sensitive and unemotional
	Sincere and loyal to loved ones
	Uncomplaining
	Purposeful and determined

When the Emperor performed the annual sacrifices to Shang-Ti, the Supreme God he would offer the final sacrifice which would be a young Bull (Bilsky, 1975). While the Bull was the expected sacrifice in other ceremonies, the Sheep was an accepted substitute. The ancient sacrifice of the Ox must be due to the important role the beast plays in agriculture.

The Ox features in several types of sacrifices. In many parts of ancient China, human sacrifices were eventually replaced by cattle sacrifices (Eberhard, 1968, p.342).

The Bull was an ancient symbol of power, fertility and strength in ancient Egypt. It was supposed to represent exceptional "fertilizing force." It was worshipped at Memphis as Mnevis sacred to the sun and at Heliopolis as Apis sacred to the moon. In ancient Crete it was an important symbol of the sun (both were generative forces). Together with the Ram, the Bull was also associated with Zeus to whom both the Bull and Ram would be sacrificed (Whittick, 1960, p.154).

The Cow is a symbol of procreation associated with Isis (or Hathor) the sister of Osiris and mother of Horus. Hathor was the goddess of procreation and supposed to be the mother of the race. In Greece, the Cow is the symbol of Hera, the wife of Zeus (Whittick, 1960, p.163).

The Egyptian Osiris and Horus are said to have Bull heads. Osiris is the Egyptian god of Hell or the Underworld. The Chinese Hell god, Yim-kan, is also said to have a Bull-head. The famous Horse-Bull deities guard the Gate of Hell.

The Ox is an ancient symbol of wealth, probably related to its being a medium of exchange prior to metal and coins as well an ancient animal of sacrifice in many cultures (Whittick, 1960, p.232).

The Indian said that seeing a Bull or Buffalo sitting or moving on the road towards his right, it is good. But two Buffaloes crossing from the right to the left is bad.

ASTROLOGICAL SIGNIFICANCE

The second of the Zodiacal Animals, whose astrological characteristics are illustrated in Table 13.1 and 13.2.

The Ox is the domestic equivalent of the Centre Heraldic Animal, the Golden *Lung*. It is also the ninth constellation, *Niu* the Ox. The *Tong-Shu* describes it as falling on a Friday under the influence of the planet Venus and being inauspicious:

> Building today will damage the charm of pretty ladies and will lead to brothers quarrelling like wolves and tigers. Marriages and burials will cause luck to disappear and make the family emigrate.

The Ox is associated with the Immortal Lao Tzu riding the Ox in his search for immortality among the mountains. It is also associated with the Divine Cowherd (Figure 13.1).

14

THE HARE OR RABBIT

Link with: Three-legged Frog or Toad

HISTORICAL BACKGROUND

The Chinese have two species of Hare, one living north and the other south of the Yangtze River. The former is a true *lepus* while the other is a *caprolagus*. Both do not burrow holes but take shelters in others' homes.

The Hare or Rabbit is supposed to be the servant of a genie and uses a pestle to pound drugs composing the elixir of life under a sacred *cassia* tree on the moon. This Moon Hare or Jade Rabbit is sometimes pictured with the Three-Legged Frog or Toad or pounding the elixir on the head of the Toad.

The pounding Rabbit is associated with Chang-O, Moon Goddess and both are supposed to live on the Moon (Figure 14.1). Chang-O sometimes assumes the form of the Three-Legged Toad. At times, this Rabbit is accompanied by the Woodcutter who is doomed forever to try to cut down the magic *cassia* tree.

During the Lantern Festival of the Eighth Moon, shops would stock lanterns of all shapes, especially those of Rabbits. They would also be other rabbit toys.

AUSPICIOUS MEANINGS OF RABBIT

Since the legends associate the moon Rabbit with the elixir of life, it naturally symbolizes longevity.

Like the western Beer Rabbit, forever outwitting Beer Fox, the Hare is considered by the Chinese as a genius and nobody would hunt it. The Chinese look on it, especially the red variety, as a divine animal. White Hares are omens of good luck and their appearance is a mark of heavenly approval. The red Hare is auspicious and appears only when rulers of the Empire are virtuous.

Figure 14.1: The Moon Rabbit or Hare.
It is associated with Chang-O, the Moon goddess. It symbolizes
longevity. White Hares are signs of good luck.

It is also the symbol of supreme self-sacrifice, from the legend of the Buddha Hare (see below).

ASTROLOGICAL SIGNIFICANCE

The fourth of the Zodiacal Animals, whose astrological characteristics are illustrated in Table 14.1. It is also the fourth constellation, Fang the Room (Table 2.3). The *Tong-Shu* says that it falls on a Sunday under the influence of the Sun and is auspicious:

> To build today brings abundant wealth and prosperity. The Gods of Happiness, Longevity, Honour, Riches and Glory hasten to see you. Funerals held today will lead to officials promoted three ranks.

AUSPICIOUS LEGENDS ABOUT RABBIT

While the Rabbit is linked with the tragic tale of Chang-O the Moon Goddess, its character could also be illustrated by the story of the Buddha Hare .

The Buddha Hare

The Buddha was once a Hare in a former reincarnation. The Hare was the wisest of animals and he was particularly followed by a Crocodile, a Monkey and a Fox. The Hare told his followers that hospitality was most important in the world and that all of them should be prepared to entertain hosts. Indra the king of gods decided to test the animals and went down as a wandering hermit. The Crocodile invited the hermit to eat the food it had stored. The Monkey gave the hermit the nuts. The Fox let the hermit ate the food it had stored. But when Indra visited the Hare it had nothing. However, the Hare told the hermit to prepare a fire as food was acoming. When the fire was ready and the pot was boiling the Hare jumped into the pot to serve as food for the hermit. But Indra through his magic powers prevented the Hare from being boiled alive and praised the Hare for its self-sacrifice.

Table 14.1

The Zodiacal Significance Of Hare

Terrestrial Branches Significance

Order of Animals:	4th
Time ruled by Hare:	4th Hour, Mao (0500 to 0700)
Month	4th Moon
Year	1903, 1915, 1927, 1939, 1951, 1963, 1975, 1987
Season	Mid Spring
Direction	East
Western constellation	Pisces
Ruling Planet	Jupiter
Lucky Gemstone	Chrysolites
Shade	Yin
Symbol:	Symbol of Longevity with Virtue and Prudence.
Good points:	Calm, discreet, gentle, reserved. Gracious and good mannered. Intelligent, farsighted, very intuitive and methodical. Good memory. Makes wise counsellor. Knack of doing business.
Bad points:	Indecisive, not always fair, moody, touchy, suspicious, worldly. Not faithful in love as he has a taste for sex.
Others:	Will have tranquil life of peace and congeniality. Lucky in business.
Compatible	Sheep, Dog, Boar
Incompatible	Cock, Tiger, Horse

Table 14.2

Effects Of Tiangan Factor on Zodiac Significance Of Hare

The *tiangan* factor would predispose the Hare along the following trends:

Metal   Sturdier than other Hares
Self-confident of own intelligence
Preoccupied with own desires and goals
Connoisseur of good things
Dark moods
Ardent in love
Many hidden inhibitions

Water   Mediative
Fragile emotional
Excellent memory
Subjective, not decisive, indulge in self-pity
Suspicious, overimaginative

Wood   Generous, understanding, too charitable
for own good
Intimidated by authority
Work well in groups, but bureaucratic

Fire   Intuitive, psychic
Demonstrative, fun loving, affectionate
Easy going and natural
Discreet and moderate
Avoid confrontation with enemies
Easily moved to anger and disappointment

Earth   Serious, steadfast
Deliberative and calculative
Balanced and rational
Constant, less indulgent
Introvert, humble enough to see own shortcomings
Materialistic

THE HORSE

HISTORICAL BACKGROUND

The Horse is originally a native of Central Asia. It is the last of the animals to be domesticated on account of its unruly nature. Until recently, the Horse features predominantly in battles and agriculture. Today, the Chinese find Horse-racing a fascinating gambling game.

The bones of Horses, Sheep and cattle were not commonly found in China until 1400BC during the Shang dynasty (even though the ancient Chinese records mention Horses much earlier than the Shang dynasty). This indicates that these animals were introduced into China from the West, possibly through migration of people from the West into ancient China.

Horses feature in many cave paintings as mere scrawls. It seems that originally Horses were hunted as game only. But the first culture to ride and harness the Horse were the Chinese. The Chinese were also the first to exploit it. However, the most ancient script about Horse training was that of the Hittite Empire (1360BC) composed for their chariot corps. Earlier, around 1750BC, the Hittites swept through Egypt then Babylon and Assyria and then the Near East owing to the advantages of their war-chariots drawn by Horses (Saures, 1979, pp.4, 16).

In ancient China, the Horse replaced the cattle as animals drawing carts in the time of Emperor Yu (Hsu and Ward, 1984, p.70; Eberhard, 1968). By Han's times, the use of the Horse-drawn war chariots was eliminated.

The Chinese character for Horse *Ma* is a pictorial figure of the animal, showing the maned head and the four legs. A famous story is about the Eight Horses of Mu Wang (1001-746BC) the fifth Emperor of the Chou Dynasty. The eight Horses were the chariot Horses of King Mu as he was driven by his charioteer through the empire (Williams, 1931, p.191).

Figure 15.1: The Horse-drawn Chariot.
The Horse, often depicted in lively forms, symbolizes speed and perseverance.

The Manchu, who loved Horses so much, used the Horse for their court dress. The sleeves of their officials were shaped like Horse's hooves while the famous cue, hated by all patriotic Chinese, was representative of the Horse-tail.

It may be surprising to many to realize that the Chinese Herbal *Pen Ts' ao* actually prescribes the Horse for medicinal purposes. The pure white Horses are best for medicine. Such Horses should not drink from a Hog's water trough and Monkeys should be kept from them otherwise the Horses will get their diseases. Only the liver of the Horse is poisonous. The heart is good for forgetfulness.

AUSPICIOUS MEANINGS OF HORSE

The galloping Horse, so full of energy, is an emblem of speed and perseverance. The popular painting of "one hundred colts" is really the symbol of the quick-witted youth.

It is also the symbol of high official status, as depicted in a drawing of two Monkeys and a Horse. The Monkey's name *Hou* could means *Monkey* and also Lord. Hence, the pun means noble rank.

Emperor Yu was said to replace the cattle-drawn carts with Horses (Eberhard, 1968). The Horse-drawn chariot (Figure 15.1) is a symbol of high official position. People would make the wish:

> May your generations ride in chariots.

Horses reared in the presence of Monkeys are said to do well. (q.v. Monkey). This is probably due to the famous story of *Journey to the West* where the Monkey God is once a Guardian of the Heavenly stable of Horses.

· The Horse's skull would calm the restless and hysterical mind and is also a charm. This charm's properties are attributed to the hooves of the Horse hung in a house – the probable origin of the good luck Horse shoe nailed to the door. A

Horse's hoof on the roof of a house preserves the house against the dead. But Chinese reverence for the dead often prevent them from putting up such a charm (Dennys, 1968, p.48)

The Horse symbolizes strength, courage and also death and the swiftness of life. It is associated with Poseidon (or the Sea God Neptune). It also symbolizes the passage from one existence to another. (Whittick, 1960, p.199). Ma Wang, the King of Horses, is an ugly ogre with three eyes and four hands with weapons. He is usually accompanied by a similar figure of the King of Oxen. These two deities, originally deities protecting Horses and cattle, also feature as the two animal escorts who guide all dead souls to the Judgement Hall of Hell.

The Book of Lu Pan with its twenty-seven magic pictures associates the Horse with military greatness (Eberhard, 1970):

A man, a Horse, a lance, renown in military service and great happiness. The name becomes well-known in the world, the barbarians surrender; death as a general in the field.

ASTROLOGICAL SIGNIFICANCE

The seventh of the Zodiacal Animals, whose astrological characteristics are illustrated in Table 15.1 and Table 15.2.

It is the twenty-fifth lunar constellation, Hsing the Seven Stars in Hydra (Table 2.3). The *Tong-Shu* says that it falls on a Sunday under the influence of the sun and is inauspicious:

Today is good for building houses and prosperity will lead one to the feet of the Emperor. But a funeral or irrigating the paddy field will cause the wife to abandon the husband for another man.

Table 15.1

The Zodiacal Significance Of Horse

Terrestrial Branches Significance

Order of Animals:	7th
Time ruled by Horse	7th Hour, Wu (1100 to 1300)
Month	7th moon
Year	1906, 1918, 1930, 1942, 1954, 1966, 1978, 1990
Season	Mid Summer
Direction	South
Western constellation	Gemini
Ruling Planet	Mercury
Lucky Gemstone	Beryl
Shade	Yang
Symbol:	Eight Horses of Happiness and Distinguished Career
Good points:	Lively, cheerful, very sociable, Quick, elegant, kindly though quick tempered. Independent, loves travels, changes and usually quickly leaves home. Makes friends easily and helpful, loyal. Clever perceptive but not exactly intelligent. Good at promoting grand ideas.
Bad points:	Impulsive and stubborn. Takes little of others' advice, weak and susceptible in love. Inconsistent because of moods, talks too much and cannot keep secrets. Opportunistic, self-centred, boastful, ostentatious, irritable. Tend to rush people but unable to stick to schedules.
Others:	Better life if born at winter
Compatible	Tiger, Dog, Sheep
Incompatible	Rat, Ox

Table 15.2

Effects Of Tiangan Factor on Zodiac Significance Of Horse

The *tiangan* factor would predispose the Horse along the following trends:

Metal	Prolific and intuitive mind
	Popular but unruly
	Demonstrative, impetus, bold
	Looking for new experience
	Strongly recuperative
	Stubborn, self-centered
Water	Excellent business acumen
	Cheerful, adaptable
	Restless, nomadic type
	Change mind too often, inconsistent, inconsiderate
	Humorous, dressful
Wood	Disciplined, systematic
	Friendly, cooperative
	Happy disposition, sociable
	Progressive, unsentimental, modern
	High spirited
Fire	Flamboyant with personal magnetism
	Superb intellect, ingenious, resourceful
	Inconsistent, no perseverance
	Volatile
	Loves travel, action, thrill and changes
Earth	Happy, congenial
	Logical, less decisive, slow moving
	Offer least resistance to authority, careful
	Hedges decisions

Note that the Horse's astrological direction is South which is the heraldic position of the Phoenix. Part of a Chinese song, The Ten Connected Numbers (Eberhard,

1970), has: Four Horses team up with the T'ang, four Phoenixes welcome the son, the four great *vajras* ...

The Horse is more auspicious in the West than in the East and seldom feature much in Chinese mythology. A probable reason is that its alternate, the Phoenix, has taken up much of the associated meanings.

THE SHEEP

Link with: Domestic equivalent of Azure Lung

HISTORICAL BACKGROUND

The Sheep (Figure 16.1), along with the Horse and cattle, were seldom found in China until around 1400BC. It was evidently introduced from the West.

Sheep in the western parts as in Liao-tung are white or pale colour in contrast to black Pigs, while those in the east like in Kiang-nan they are black or dark colour in contrast to white or pale Pigs.

The Chinese character for Sheep preserved the component for *Wang* the three horizontal strokes with a vertical cross stroke. This character *Wang* is a fire from the earth and denotes the ancient sacrificial fire – originally *Wang* was associated with the priest who was also the ruler. The Sheep, incorporating this "Wang" component, was thus an ancient sacrificial animal.

AUSPICIOUS MEANINGS OF SHEEP

It is the emblem of retired life. The Lamb is a symbol of filial piety as it kneels to receive nourishment from its dame.

In times of drought it is considered as a felicitous animal and is carried in processions with dancing and music.

In ancient China, the Sheep as a common sacrificial animal, was an accepted substitute for the young Bull in certain ceremonies. If the Sheep was not available, the Pig was an accepted substitute. When sacrificed, it is a memorial of resignation as it dies without a sound of protest.

The Lamb, used in ancient times for sacrifices, is the symbol of Christ. Generally it symbolizes innocence, gentleness, meekness (quite like the Dove). The Lamb also represents the young of God's people. (Whittick, 1960, p.203)

The Sheep is also the symbol of Christ's care for His followers. The Good Shepherd with his flock of Sheep was a common Christian symbol on catatombs, paintings, sarcophagi, lamps, etc. (Whittick, 1960, p.261)

Figure 16.1: The Goat or Sheep.
The Goat or Sheep is the symbol of retired life. The Lamb is the symbol of filial piety. Just like the Ox, the Goat or Sheep is a common sacrificial animal.

Table 16.1

The Zodiacal Significance Of Sheep

Terrestrial Branches Significance

Order of Animals:	8th
Time ruled by Sheep	8th Hour, Wei (1300 to 1500)
Month	8th moon
Year	1907, 1919, 1931, 1943, 1955, 1967, 1979, 1991
Season	End of Summer
Direction	S30W
Western constellation	Cancer
Ruling Planet	Moon
Lucky Gemstone	Emerald
Shade	Yin
Symbol:	Social success and distinguished career
Good points:	Easy going, sweet, gentle, compassionate. Dislike strict discipline. Fond of children and nature. Artistic, creative, fashionable. Affectionate.
Bad points:	Easily overcome by emotions, tiresome oblique habit, pessimistic, Indecisive and dependent. Not methodical. Troubled superficial love and off-hand marriage.
Others:	Fantastic luck. But will need strong loyal friends to lean on.
Compatible	Horse, Pig, Tiger
Incompatible	Rat
Others:	Ox, Dog

Table 16.2

Effects Of Tiangan Factor on Zodiac Significance Of Sheep

The *tiangan* factor would predispose the Sheep along the following trends:

Metal   Great faith and confidence in himself.
Vulnerable ego, easily hurt.
Artistic .
Family orientated and socially limited.
Unstable emotions, possessive, jealous.

Water   Not really knowledgeable.
Extremely appealing to others, popular.
Opportunistic.
Will not try new things, take majority view.
Martyrdom or persecution complex.

Wood   Thoughtful, good humoured.
Sentimental, compassionate and pleasing.
High morals.
Trusting and liable to be taken advantage of.
Tend to mother those whom he loves.
People will help him in need.

Fire   Courageous, initiative.
Sure footed.
Tend to dramatize, energetic, aggressive.
Over indulgent and mismanage financial matters.
Wistful thinker, sullen and spiteful.

Earth   Optimistic self reliant.
Conservative, careful.
Domestically loyal.
Work and play hard.
Neurotic, defensive.

The Ram is an ancient Egyptian, Greek and Roman symbol of procreation and fertility. Amen was the chief Egyptian god around the twelfth dynasty – he was a creative god with hidden force and power of creation. The Ram was associated with Amen who would be represented with a Ram's head. Amen-Ra was the Theban Zeus, who at times had the Ram's horns. Sacred to Zeus it was often an animal of sacrifice. The Ram's head on the sepulchral altar also expresses eternal life by an extension of the idea of vital life force. A Roman inscription on an altar with a Ram decoration speaks of rebirth to life eternal (Whittick, 1960, p.243)

In some parts of northern China, sickness could be dispelled by calling in a sorceress who would perform a "Sheep Dance" beating an iron drum covered with sheepskin.

ASTROLOGICAL SIGNIFICANCE

The eighth of the Zodiacal Animals, whose astrological characteristics are illustrated in Table 16.1 and Table 16.2.

It is the domestic equivalent of the East Heraldic Animal, Azure *Lung* (Table 2.2) It is also the twenty-third constellation, *Kuei* the Imp (Table 2.3). The *Tong-Shu* describes it as falling on Friday under the influence of Venus and being inauspicious:

To build today will lead to disappearance of the master. Funerals will bring advancement but marriages will end with the lady being lonely.

THE MONKEY

HISTORICAL BACKGROUND

The Monkey is most well-known in Chinese fables as the mischievous but delightful Monkey God, Sun Wu-Kong, though the legend does not do full credit to the true significance of the Monkey God.

The Monkey was used in dance performances in the Han dynasty. It was also a food delicacy, especially the soup of its head. The skin of the golden brown Monkey, *Rhinopethicus roxellanae*, was valuable and supposed to be worn only by members of the Imperial family.

Many things are attributed to the Monkey; for example it could talk, it knew the past, it is like a man. There are stories that the Monkey could kidnap women and sent them back when pregnant (Eberhard, 1968, pp.50-52).

AUSPICIOUS MEANINGS OF MONKEY

The symbol of the Monkey holding in its hand a peach is said to bring long life. (Figure 17.1).

The Monkey is believed to control hobgoblins, witches, elves, etc. Thus, it would confer health, protection and success through keeping off these evil spirits. The Monkey God may be worshipped to drive away or prevent evil influences from the spirits.

Horse reared in presence of Monkeys are said to do well.

It is also an emblem of ugliness and trickery. In the *Journey to the West*, the Monkey is a symbol of human intelligence and of man's skill and resourcefulness. The nickname "Monkey King" is given to a cunning man. In the *Journey to the West* the Monkey is also adept in medicine.

Figure 17.1 : The Monkey.
The Monkey holding the Peach is a symbol of long life. The
Monkey also gives protection against evil spirits and confers
health and success.
"The Journey to the West" is a Ming story built around the jour-
ney of a Tang priest purported to be escorted by the Monkey God,
the Pig spirit and the Mountain Sand Priest. But legends about the
Monkey God existed long before the Tang dynasty. He is known as
Hanuman in the Indian legend of the Ramayana. For example,
Sun Wu-Kong, the Monkey God was well-versed in medicine, a
fighter of evil and was supposed to be the sworn brother of
Emperor Huang-Ti of 2600BC.

The Indian says that a man on a journey seeing a Monkey by his left side or on the right side of the road is good. Seeing a Monkey at twilight means the man would achieve his aims.

ASTROLOGICAL SIGNIFICANCE

It is the ninth Zodiacal Animals, whose astrological characteristics are illustrated in Table 17.1 and Table 17.2. The animal is the twentieth constellation, *Tzu* the Bristle (Monkey) and also the twenty-first constellation, *Shen*, to Mix (Ape) (Table 2.3). The *Tong-Shu* describes:

> Twentieth constellation, also the Turtle, falling on a Tuesday under the influence of Mars and inauspicious: Build today will bring lawsuit. A funeral will lead to collapse of the house with at least three deaths to follow and food reserves will dwindle.

> Twenty-first constellation, also the Three Associates, falling on a Wednesday under the influence of Mercury and auspicious: Build today and prosperity will come. The star of a lettered man will give light. Irrigating the paddy field and business will be fruitful. But marriages and funerals will break up the family.

The Song of the Ten Numbers quotes: "great king in the seventh heaven is the king of the monkeys" (Eberhard, 1970, p.161).

It is associated with the famous Monkey God, who is also the Great Sage Equal of Heaven or the Handsome White Monkey King (Wu Cheng-An, Ming dynasty). The Monkey God birthday is on the twenty-third day of the second Chinese moon. This is very close to the birthday of Kuan Yin the Goddess of Mercy on nineteenth day of the second Moon. These are related to the legend of the introduction of the Buddhist scriptures into China from India, as told in the story *Journey to the West*. Erh Lang, the Mountain God who helped captured Monkey, also has his birthday on the third day of the second moon.

Table 17.1

The Zodiacal Significance Of Monkey

Terrestrial Branches Significance

Order of Animals:	9th
Time ruled by Monkey	9th Hour, Shen (1500 to 1700BC)
Month	9th moon
Year	1908, 1920, 1932, 1944, 1956, 1968, 1980, 1992
Season	Early Autumn
Direction	S60W
Western constellation	Leo
Ruling Planet	Sun
Lucky Gemstone	Emerald
Shade	Yang
Symbol:	Intelligence and Resourcefulness
Good points:	Lively superior complex.
	Likes jokes, restless.
	Agile, diplomatic.
	Intelligent, inventive, with good memory.
	Charming, flexible, competitive.
	Resistant to insults.
Bad points:	Dishonest, selfish.
	Inconsistent.
	Have little respect for others.
	Easily jealous and yields easily to temptations.
	All life always difficult.
Others:	Good if born in summer.
Compatible	Rat, Dragon
Incompatible	Snake, Tiger

AUSPICIOUS LEGENDS OF MONKEY

The Monkey is featured in many Chinese mythologies, the most famous being *Journey to the West* which is 100-chapter long (Wu Cheng-An, Ming dynasty). Several tales reflect the Monkey's trickery and passion for women and wine.

Table 17.2

**Effects Of Tiangan Factor
On Zodiac Significance Of Monkey**

The "tiangan" factor would predispose the Monkey along the following trends:

Metal   Strong, sophisticated, independent.
               Wise in investment. Fighting type, hardworking.
               Consistent, practical.
               Ardent, demonstrative in affection.
               Warm, positive. Creative, trend-setter.
               Self-conscious and proud.

Water   Cooperative, speculative.
               Kind, pleasant. Secretive, devious.
               Takes offence easily. Flair, original.
               Understanding of human relationship.
               Vacillative, erratic.

Wood   Good communication, orderly.
               Honorable and prestigious.
               Intuitive, forward looking, Careful

Fire   Energetic, gesticulating
               Natural leader and innovative
               Self-assured, determined, expressive, bold
               Vitality, forceful, tends to dominate others
               Fertile imagination but not careful. Lucky in risks
               Competitive, prone to jealousy and suspicions
               Opinionated, stubborn

Earth   Placid, reliable, cool. Expansive, charitable
               Intellectual, studious, well read
               Honest, straightforward.
               Kind, devoted, dutiful, unselfish
               Not fond of entertaining
               Demands appreciation or he will sulks

MONKEY AS ANCESTOR OF CHOU DYNASTY

A Monkey is reputed to marry the female servant of the daughter of Heaven and became the ancestor of the Ch'i people in China; another is that it likewise became the ancestor of the Cheng people. Cheng being a name for northern Chinese (Eberhard, 1968, p.51). Another Monkey clan is the Yang clan who is found in southwest China, in Shu and is possibly related to the Tibetan people (Eberhard, 1968, p.52). It is interesting to note that the Chou dynasty is said to descend from the great Ch'i people too, thereby making the Monkey an ancestor of the Chou dynasty (Eberhard, 1968, p.53).

THE MONKEY GOD LEGEND

Sun Wu-Kong was born out of a magic stone and soon gain magical powers after being trained by the Taoist Immortal P'u-Ti Tsu-shih. He managed to obtain the magic pole of Yu from intimidating the Dragon King. He became the leader of the monkeys and assumed leadership position among the animals of the earth. Not satisfied, Sun Wu-Kong demanded and got positions from Heaven, including the title of Great Sage Equal to Heaven. Sun Wu-Kong moved from one capricious act to another, including stealing and eating the peaches of immortality of the Queen of Heaven, until the host of heaven was sent to capture him. Though captured, the Monkey could not be destroyed by Heaven nor even by Lao Tzu's furnace of the Eight Diagrams. However, the Goddess of Mercy was able to trick and trap the Monkey under a magic mountain to await the coming of the priest, Hsuan Tsang, who fetched the Buddhist scriptures from India. What follows is the famous story where the Monkey, along with the Pig Spirit and the Mountain Hermit, assisted the priest through a series of adventures to fetch the scriptures.

Journey to the West is a Ming tale of the Tang Emperor commissioning a trip to the West to obtain the Sacred Buddhist Scriptures. The Ming tale is a collection of tales, some of which are known to exist long before the Tang dynasty. The historic event of the Tang mission to obtain the Buddhist Scriptures was used to thread the odd tales into a delightful story.

Hsuan Tsang the priest himself is related to the legend of Madam White Snake (q.v. Snake) where he is actually the filial son of Madam White Snake.

It is evident that the Chinese have borrowed the significance from the famous Indian tale of the Ramayana where Hanuman the Monkey King aided Rama against the Ravanna the Dragon King. The fight between Hanuman and Ravanna the Dragon King finds parallel in the Chinese tale where Sun Wu-Kong, the Monkey God, went into the ocean to force the Dragon King to yield to him the famous magic pole of Yu.

Who exactly is the Monkey God, Sun Wu-Kong?

THE LINK BETWEEN MONKEY
AND EMPEROR TA YU

There is a significant link between the Monkey God and Yu, which would reveal the identity of the Monkey God, despite the caricature built around him due to *Journey to the West*.

The *Yu* who used the magic pole of Yu to level the grounds when combating the ancient floods is the Third and last Sage Emperor Ta Yu, the founder of the legendary Hsia dynasty. Burkhardt (1982, p.172) mentions that it was the Jade Emperor who placed the pole to gauge the tide.

According to the *Shan Hai Ching*, when Yu was taming the floods, he chained the water animal causing the damage. This animal had escaped from a previous chaining to the Tortoise Mountain (Eberhard, 1968, pp.60-61). This water animal or god was said to be the Monkey, or in other versions as the Rhinoceros or even the Cattle. This animal was so fierce that Yu had to call in many helpers to capture it.

THE BIRTH OF MONKEY FROM A STONE

One of the most significant aspects of the legend of the Monkey God is that he was born out of a stone. Chang (1983, pp.10-11) records this legend about Yu's birth:

Yu, founder of the Hsia dynasty, and the clan's ancestor appeared to have been born out of a rock. Yu's father, Kun, charged with stemming a great flood, stole the swelling mold from the Supreme God. With this he built dams which through their swelling would hold back the waters but his efforts failed. The Supreme God, angered by his theft, had him executed. His body remained for three years as a stone. Then somebody cut it open with a sword, then Yu emerged from his father's belly. Another story is that when Yu was digging a passage through a mountain, he changed into a bear. His wife, the Lady of Tu Shan, saw him, ran away and she changed to a stone. She was pregnant then. When Yu ran after her and shouted: "Give me my son!" the stone split open at its north side and a child named Ch'i came forth.

Emperor Ta Yu, the founder of the Hsia dynasty, and his son are supposed to be born out of stone – similar origin as the Monkey God!

Evidently the famous story *Journey to the West* took its Monkey God from this Yu Monkey and is likely a caricature based on the combination of the feats of the Sage Emperor Yu and the Monkey. The Monkey God's title of Great Sage Equal of Heaven is appropriate of the Sage title of Emperor Ta Yu.

What is significant, too, is that Lei Kung, the Thunder God, who is usually depicted as a bird-like deity, also has a Monkey form as well as an alternate Bear-Pig form with fleshy wings (Eberhard, 1968, pp.253-254). The Pakua

Thunder Magic dance of Taoism, used against black magic, is sometimes known as the Dance or Steps of Yu. This is reminiscent of the Bear Dance of *Fang Siang-Che* dance described earlier in Chapter 2, which is used to combat serious calamities believed to be caused by spiritual disorders.

The Dance of Yu, which was used to control the floods (Chang, 1983, p.45), is also a dance depicting the crane killing the snakes. Another name for this dance is the Bear dance (Eberhard, 1968, p.74) where Yu is said to take the form of a Bear while performing the dance (Eberhard, 1968, p.259). This is similar to the Pakua Thunder Magic or Phoenix destroying the Serpent behind the black magic!

Yu is also associated with the water animal, the Tortoise (q.v.) (Eberhard, 1968, p.199). This water animal is also said to be a Bear. It is interesting to note that Yu, or rather his father Kun, is also said to have a Pig form and was connected with the one-eye giant Fang-Seng (Eberhard, 1968, pp.350-357); this could be the reason for the inclusion of the Pig God and the Mountain Hermit monster in the story *Journey to the West*.

These connections between the Monkey to the Sage Emperor Yu and the Thunder God would explain the manifold significance of the Monkey in Chinese culture.

THE FOWL: COCKS AND HENS

Linked with: Domestic equivalent of Phoenix, Crane

HISTORICAL BACKGROUND

The Fowl is a common food item among many countries, including China. The Blackbones Fowls are prized for making soups for people with gastric problems. Adopting the principle of *Yin-Yang* balance, female birds are prepared for the male patient and male birds for the female patient.

AUSPICIOUS MEANINGS OF COCKEREL

Auspiciousness is generally ascribed to the Cock (Figure 18.1) rather than the Hen. However, the Hen has some auspicious significance attached to it.

The Cock and Hen together among rocks is a symbol of the pleasantness of country life. Despite the connection of the Fowl to the tenth Moon, the Cock and Hen are also the birds of the second Moon. Plum and chickens augur the period.

COCK

The Cock is the domestic equivalent of the Phoenix, the South Heraldic Animal. As such much of the Cock's auspiciousness are similar to those of the Phoenix.

The Cock's crow means "Happiness to our nation" and also "Eastern skies are reddening" – red being the lucky colour (Bowie). His crowing in the morning is supposed to scare off the evil spirits.

During the fifth day of the fifth moon, the Pakua over the five Poisonous Animals – Snake, Scorpion, Spider, Centipede and Toad, would be put over the door to ward off evil. Sometimes, instead of the Pakua, there would be the image of a huge red Cock killing the poisonous animals.

Figure 18.1: The Cock.
Auspicious as a sacrificial animal of oaths. It symbolizes the Sun
and the warmth and life of the Universe.

Table 18.1

**The Zodiacal Significance Of Cockerel
Terrestrial Branches Significance**

Order of Animals:	10th
Time ruled by Cock	10th Hour, Yu (1700 to 1900)
Month	10th moon
Year	1909, 1921, 1933, 1945, 1957, 1969, 1981, 1993
Season	Mid Autumn
Direction	West
Western constellation	Virgo
Ruling Planet	Mercury
Lucky Gemstone	Pink Jasper
Shade	Yin
Symbol:	Red Cock frightens off demons, who flees at sight of his red comb.
Good points:	Honest, Very intelligent, thinker, excellent memory, alert and organized. Interesting, above average. Generous as a friend. Attractive. Confident, outstanding performer. Clever at finance.
Bad points:	Boastful, show-off. Easily critical, opinionated and misunderstood.
Compatible	Snake, Ox, Dragon.
Incompatible	Dog, Rat, Rabbit.

The Cock is an embodiment of the *Yang* and represents the warmth and life of the universe. It can change into human form to inflict good or bad on mortals. The Cock also symbolizes Five Virtues:

- Literary spirit crown
- War spirit spurs
- Courage always fight his enemies

- Benevolent always clucking for Hens when he finds a grain
- Faithful never fail to tell the hour

Table 18.2

Effects Of Tiangan Factor
on Zodiac Significance Of Cockerel

The *tiangan* factor would predispose the Cockerel along the following trends:

Metal	Practical, exacting, industrious Optimistic, idealistic Opinionated, headstrong Good at oratory Inwardly inhibitory, orderly in life Materialistic but concern with social issues.
Water	Thinking intellectual. Energetic, initiative. Proficient in speaking Strong in technology
Wood	Progress orientated Considerate, less opinionated, fair Honest, with integrity Sociable Reliable
Fire	Vigorous, authoritative Diligent, intense Temperamental, over-dramatic Strongly principled, ethical, independent and good manager Can be inflexible
Earth	Studious, analytical Accurate, efficient, systematic Outspoken, critical Unpretentious, dogmatic Hard taskmaster, strict

During a marriage, after the worship of Heaven and Earth a table would be set out and fruits placed on top of a platter of willow wood which is supposed to have supernatural powers. These fruits compose of two small white Cocks made of sugar, five kinds of dry fruits, a bundle of chopsticks, a foot measure, a mirror, a pair of shears and a case containing money scales. The items are omens of prosperity and future harmony. The shears are a symbol of industry, the mirror a kind of protection against divination. It is customary for the bridegroom and bride to eat the white sugar Fowls. The double Cocks may be another way to symbolize the Dragon-Phoenix pair which is the symbol of harmony and richness of marriages.

The white Cock or its image is also placed on coffins to lure the soul of the departed to enter it, and also to drive away demons which would otherwise harm the dead soul. It is said that one of the three spirits of the dead would enter the body of the Cock as it met the corpse and this spirit could then be lured back into the home of the family. The Cock has to be white as it symbolizes purity of heart. The white Cock is said to be a protection against baneful astral influences and is the only capable guide of the transient spirits. Note: The white crane is also placed on coffins for similar reasons.

The Cock is also a Christian symbol for vigilance and is thus placed at summits of towers and steeples. It is associated as an emblem of the Passion and with Peter as repentance. In Greece it is symbolic of Persephone's rising in the spring (Whittick, 1960, p.160).

The Cockerel is auspicious to the Chinese as the sacrificial bird of oaths and should not be slain on ordinary occasions. The flesh of the male bird is said to be injurious.

The Cock generally crows early in the morning to welcome the day. If a Cock crows about ten or eleven in the morning it is an unlucky sign for the family. The Cock is not allowed to stay with the family and would be either killed or sold.

HENS

Hens are common sacrificial animals. The principle here is that the sins of the people are transferred to the entrails of the hens which were placed on rooftops to be carried away by the birds of the air. This custom is quite similar to those of the Jews.

Crowing Hens indicate subversion in the family and the emblem of petticoat government dominated by eunuch:

> A whistling woman and crowing hen, are not fit for gods or men.

The Hen crowing is an ominous indication that something unusual is going to happen to the owners' family. The position of the animal determines whether the crowing is good or bad. When the Hen's head is facing the front or the outside of the house, it is unlucky and foreshadow poverty or some ill-luck. If her head faces the rear of the house, it is considered lucky and indicates that the family would become more prosperous.

However, the crowing Hen is not popular as contrary to nature, even if the omen is good, it is not desirable. The bird would be immediately killed or sold.

Setting a Hen on an even number of eggs would cause the Hen to be disturbed and the resultant chickens would not be thriving. Thunder during such sittings denotes an unlucky omen.

ASTROLOGICAL SIGNIFICANCE·

The Cock is the tenth of the Zodiacal Animals, whose astrological characteristics are illustrated in Table 18.1 and 18.2.

The Cock is the eighteenth lunar constellation, Mao the seven stars of Pleides. The *Tong-Shu* describes it as falling on a Sunday under the influence of the sun and that it is inauspicious:

To build on this day is to let the buffalo into the paddy field. Funerals lead to worry. To start anything will bring calamities and marriages will be miserable.

THE DOG

HISTORICAL BACKGROUND

The Dog is an indigenous animal in ancient China proper. Its bones and the bones of the Pig were found in China even before the Shang dynasty. In contrast, the bones of the cattle, Sheep and Horses were not commonly found in China until 1400BC of the Shang dynasty. As cattle, Sheep and Horses were already in the Middle East, this has led to the speculations that the Chinese civilization originated from the West. The oldest images of Dogs in China was engraved on a bronze vase of the Chou dynasty. It is classified as among the six domestic animals (birds and beasts) of China.

Its Chinese character is derived from the ancient pictogram Ch'uan and this is now the ninety-fourth radical qualifying all quadrupeds.

Pekinese Dogs (Figure 19.1) are especially favoured by the Chinese and the Imperial family kept several of them as pets. These short-legged and short-headed Dogs were mentioned in the Chou dynasty records of 1000BC. The Buddhist Lion was actually a palace Dog with lion-like characteristics and the Tibetan lamas sent Lion-Dogs as tribute to the Manchus.

It is one of the animals the Chinese would eat although many would find the idea revolting. The Chinese Almanac describes the days on which it should not be consumed (Burkhardt, 1982, p.193).

AUSPICIOUS MEANINGS OF DOG

The Dog is valued for its fidelity though despised for other purposes and serves as both guardian and scavenger. The Dog is a creature which is naturally watchful and is skilful in selection of men. In the West, the hunter and the shepherd regard the useful Dog as his friend and welcome it into the family circle. But the Chinese regards the Dog more as a burglar alarm and would often chain the animal outside.

Figure 19.1: The Pekinese Dog.
The watchful Dog is an omen of good luck. The Heavenly Dog,
whose original master was Mo Li-Shou, the angel of the North, be-
came the mascot of Erh-Lang the Mountain God.

When a strange Dog follows a person it is an omen of good luck. Should a strange Dog comes and stays with a family, it is an omen to the head that he is going to become wealthy. The Book of Five Elements say that if one breeds a black dog with white ears, he shall be rich and noble (Burkhardt, 1982, p.191). A yellow dog with white forelegs merely brings good luck, but a white with a black head brings added riches to good fortune. A white dog with black tail will cause the generations to ride in chariots.

Married women would worship the Heavenly Dog which is a genius surrounded by children. He would be shooting at a Dog in Heaven with bows and arrows. Dog is supposed to eat children of mortals. The scholar therefore protects the children of mortals. Women born during the days of the hoary character of Dog should before birth put up this picture of the scholar shooting the Heavenly Dog and burn incense. (Williams, 1931, p.103). This protector has another version where Chang Hsien is shooting at the Sky Rat (q.v. Rat) or that the genius is Chang Hsien himself (Burkhardt, 1982, p.194).

It is believed that if a hair from a Dog was mixed into a drink and that drink and the hair were swallowed, it would do good to those who had a drink too many. This idea is based on the sympathy which a part of the body has with the whole. Since the Dog's virus is powerless to harm the Dog, likewise this immunity is passed on to those who drank via the hair.

In India, it is good if a Dog with food in its mouth is seen on the right side of the road. It is also good if the Dog is scratching its head or easing itself on a rubbish heap. Dogs in coupling state are bad omens. A Cat or Dog walking over a corpse is a fearful omen. If a pregnant female animal walks over the dead, the dead will rise and pursue those nearest it and strangle anyone it catches.

Eclipses are believed to be due to the Heavenly Dog, *Tien Kou*, trying to gobble up the sun or moon. Firecrackers and banging of kitchen utensils are used to scare it off.

Table 19.1

The Zodiacal Significance Of Dog
Terrestrial Branches Significance

Order of Animals:	11th
Time ruled by Dog	11th Hour, Hsu (1900 to 2100)
Month	11th moon
Year	1910, 1922, 1934, 1946, 1958, 1970, 1982, 1994
Season	End of Autumn
Direction	N60W
Western constellation	Libra
Ruling Planet	Venus
Lucky Gemstone	Diamond
Shade	Yang
Symbol:	Wisdom and Loyalty.
Good points:	Most likable sign of the Zodiac. Great respect for "rites", moral and very honest and straightforward. Warm nature and in general esteem. Good active worker. Fighter, great sense of justice. Intelligent, intuitive, good listener, clear in judgement. Generous with a great gift for loyal friendship and likes to protect the interests of others. His anger is only short and for your sake.
Bad points:	Not happy in love, hot headed. Full of anxiety.
Others:	Better life if born at day Good Friendship owing to flair to spot hidden dangers including ambushes.
Compatible	Horse, Rabbit, Tiger
Incompatible	Cock, Dragon, Sheep.

ASTROLOGICAL SIGNIFICANCE

The Dog is the eleventh of the Zodiacal Animals, whose astrological characteristics are illustrated in Table 19.1 and Table 19.2.

Table 19.2

**Effects Of Tiangan Factor
on Zodiac Significance Of Dog**

The *tiangan* factor would predispose the Dog along the following trends:

Metal	Highest unwavering principles
	Noble and charitable
	Ruthless when aroused, stem and formidable
	Decisive and loyal
Water	Intuitive
	Attractive, easygoing
	Sympathetic, democratic
	Good counsellor, fair judge
Wood	Stable, generous
	Enchanting, amiable, popular
	Honest, considerate
	Energetic, cooperative
	Group orientated
Fire	Dramatic, buoyant, self-assured
	Attractive, magnetic charm
	Generous, honest
	Defiant and rebellious if forced to do things
	Fierce when attacked
	Adventurous, creative
Earth	Idealistic and tends to overperform
	Impartial adviser
	Efficient, constructive worker
	Vigilant and careful
	Quiet, kind hearted, but secretive
	Good fighter and survivor

It is also the sixteenth constellation, Lou the Mound or Link (Table 2.3). The *Tong-Shu* describes it as falling on a Friday under the influence of Venus and being auspicious:

> Building today is like building the gates of Heaven; the family will be richer and everything will prosper and there will be many joys. Funerals will lead to social promotions and marriages will lead to complete harmony.

AUSPICIOUS LEGENDS OF DOG

The Dog, in common with the Tigers, Wolves and Foxes, seems to be associated with demons. According to a tale, in the Lin-lu mountain existed an arbour inhabited by a demon and its numerous companions. These demonic companions were really dogs transformed into human beings. Whoever passed the night with them was sure to die.

Other more auspicious stories include those of the *Tien Kou* and Pan Hu below.

THE HEAVENLY DOG OF ERH-LANG

The Heavenly Dog, *Tien Kou*, was originally the pet of the angel Mo Li-Shou, Spirit General of the North (otherwise the Black Snake or Tortoise), who kept it in his dog-bag. It could change its sizes and turn to as big as an elephant and bite the enemies with its razor sharp teeth. But it made the mistake of swallowing the Chou general, Erh Lang the Mountain God during his battle against the Mo brothers in the Chou-Shang wars. Erh Lang could not perish and the Dog was frightened with the god inside it. Erh Lang emerged and snapped it into two. Erh Lang began to take the form of this Heavenly Dog and went back to Mo Li-Shou. During the continued battles when Mo Li-Shou opened his dog bag Erh Lang bit off his hand and later Mo Li-Shou was killed by a Chou general.

After that the Heavenly Dog became the pet of Erh Lang, who used it in his battles against the Shang.

Tien Kou is worshipped by owners of pet Dogs when their Dogs are sick.

THE LEGEND OF PAN-HU

During the times of the warring Kingdoms of the dying days of the Chou dynasty, the spirit Tiger descended from heaven and gathered mighty men to harass the people of Wu. Heaven then decreed that Lou Chin-kou (Old Golden Dog) should descend to earth to tame the tiger. Heaven also ordered the Kang Chin-lung (Kang the Golden Dragon) and Niu Chin-nu (Golden Girl) to assist but not to become human beings. The Golden Dog was born into the palace of Emperor Kao-hsin at first as a golden insect. The ministers covered him with lotus leaves and nourished him for several days. The insect grew into a Dragon-Dog.

The king then announced that if anyone could bring peace to the country he would marry the third Imperial princess and he would be made an Imperial son-in-law. Only the Dragon-Dog went into the presence chamber and said he would undertake the mission. All the ministers wished him success.

Pan-Hu or Dragon-Dog turned himself into a golden Dragon and travelled for seven days and seven nights to the hall of the king of Yen. The king saw the unusual dog and took it in. He and his soldiers drank until they were intoxicated. The golden dog came and bit off the king's head and returned to Wu to report the deed.

But the king adorned another girl as a princess. Pan-Hu refused that girl and bit the hem of the third princess. Pan-Hu changed into a human form except his head which remained as a Dog head. The princess wanted to marry him.

Pan-Hu went out to war again. He crossed the river with horses and 14,000 troops and defeated the northern enemies and captured the tyrant. On return the king arranged the same day for the marriage of Pan-Hu to the third princess. Ever since, they were the ancestors of the clans of Yao.

THE PIG

HISTORICAL BACKGROUND

The Pig is a common food and sacrificial animal in China and it is not considered a hygienic animal because of the food it consumes. Many types of food products are made from this animal.

The Pig companion of the Tang priest in the story of *Journey to the West* was an incarnation of Marshall Pien, the Guardian of the Milky Way.

AUSPICIOUS MEANINGS OF PIG

The Chinese may name a person *Chu*, Pig, in the belief that evil spirits would despise that person and leave him alone.

A domestic Pig is always a good omen. It is more auspicious if the Pig is wet or covered with mud. The journeying man would achieve his objective if he sees a Pig on his left side. If the Pig is on the right side, he would still derive benefits.

The coming of the Pig into the house denotes poverty while the advent of a Dog riches. The reason is that the Pig eats and sleeps while the Dog is an industrious animal.

But, the wild Boar is a symbol of the wealth of a forest (also Figure 20.1).

The Pig is the domestic equivalent of the Snake or Tortoise, the Heraldic Animal of the North.

ASTROLOGICAL SIGNIFICANCE

The Pig is the last and twelfth of the Zodiacal Animals, whose astrological characteristics are illustrated in Table 20.1 and

Table 20.2. It is the thirteenth constellation, Shih the House (Table 2.3). The *Tong-Shu* describes it as falling on a Tuesday under the influence of Mars and being auspicious:

> Building today will lead to increase in livestock and land. Sons and grandsons will get good careers. All ventures will bring good fortunes. Marriages and funerals will remove care forever.

The third day of the Nero Year is dedicated to Pigs (Burkhardt, 1982, p.10).

Figure 20.1: The Pig.
Auspicious as a sacrificial animal.

Table 20.1

The Zodiacal Significance Of Pig

Terrestrial Branches Significance

Order of Animals:	12th
Time ruled by Pig	12th Hour, Hai (2100 to 2300)
Month	12th moon
Year	1911, 1923, 1935, 1947, 1959, 1971, 1983, 1995
Season	Early Winter
Direction	N30W
Western constellation	Scorpio
Ruling Planet	Mars
Lucky Gemstone	Topaz
Shade	yin
Symbol:	Wealth and Family prosperity, Ease. Sign attracts happiness and good fortune
Good points:	Honest, straight to the point, simple. Pure and without malice. Initiative, scrupulous, diligent. Calm, understanding, gallant. Will never hit you below the belt. Tolerant and hates disputes. A great believer of miracles.
Bad points:	Easily swindled. Wilful and obstinate Often makes mistakes and have weak arguments. Can be deprave
Others:	Better life if not born at beginning of year.
Compatible	Rabbit, Sheep, Tiger
Incompatible	Snake, Monkey

Table 20.2

Effects Of Tiangan Factor
on Zodiac Significance Of Pig

The *tiangan* factor would predispose the Pig
along the following trends:

Metal   Proud, passionate
Intense, ambitious, forceful and domineering
Very sociable and extrovert
Affectionate and can be violent
Underestimate enemies, overestimate friends
Not a quitter and lose badly

Water   Persevering and diplomatic
Perceptive and resourceful
Trusting
Cordial and peaceful
Sensuous and overindulgent

Wood   Manipulative of others with expertise,
persuasive
Charitable and good club organizer
Extremely good-hearted and can be taken
advantage of
Expansive and scrupulous

Fire   Courageous and intense
Optimistic
Love family and very generous to family
Can be wilful and a bully

Earth   Peaceful, sensible
Productive
Steady and patient
Kind and thoughtful
Devoted to family
Fond of food and drink

ANIMALS OF THE TWENTY-EIGHT CONSTELLATIONS

INTRODUCTION

In the Ganzhi System, there are also the twenty-eight *hsiu* or smaller constellations of uneven sizes. The significance of these twenty-eight constellations are not so well known as Chinese astrologers would find them complicated and tend to leave them out from the main Ganzhi System.

These Twenty-Eight Constellations are said to relate to the twenty-eight mansions of the moon and to indicate the elliptical positions and movements of the moon. But it is interesting to note that while the synodic month (from one new moon to another) is 29.53 days, the sidereal month (the period the moon takes to return to the same place among the stars) is actually 27.33 days (Needham, 1959, pp.239, 252). Needham (1959) believes that the Twenty-Eight Constellations may be a convenient average of both the synodic and sidereal month periods. But, as the Chinese astronomy is circumpolar rather than elliptical, it is likely that the Twenty-Eight Constellations are not synodic but an ill-known system based on the sidereal month.

When Matteo Ricci in AD1600s examined the then over 350 years old bronze astronomical instruments in Peking there was on each instrument the names of the Twenty-Eight Constellations (Needham, 1959, p.368). The Chinese astronomy around the Sung times was, of course, circumpolar, lending further weight to the conclusion that the Twenty-Eight Constellations are based on the sidereal and not the synodic month.

The twenty-eight *hsiu* also have their animal symbolism (Table 2.3) and are part of the sources for the significance of Chinese animal symbolism. Some of these significance have been lost and a number of the connected animals today have little significance left in the Chinese culture.

TWENTY-EIGHT CONSTELLATIONS ANIMALS ARE ASSISTANTS TO FOUR HERALDIC ANIMALS

They are related to the *tiangan* Celestial Stems system as seven *hsiu* would be allocated to each of the four quadrants of Heaven. It is evident that the animals of the Twenty-Eight Constellations are really the assistants of the Four highest groups of angels, each Group having seven main assistants. The twenty-eight animals obviously represent a lower level of angels.

Comparing with the Jewish Kabala system, the animals of these Twenty-Eight Constellations may represent the class of angels known as *Cherubims*. That is, the second highest order of angels after the *Seraphims* who are the highest angels.

There is no apparent relation between the characteristics of each of the Four Heraldic Animals with the seven animals below each of them. It is best to hold that the seven *hsiu* represent seven different aspects of the main Heraldic Animal.

TWENTY-EIGHT CONSTELLATIONS ANIMALS AS ORIGIN OF TWELVE ZODIACAL ANIMALS

It has also been believed that the Twelve Zodiacal Animals of the Terrestrial Branches system were derived from the animals of the Twenty-Eight Constellations:

- The Twelve Zodiacal Animals are among the twenty-eight animals of the Twenty-Eight Constellations.

- Figure 21.1 illustrates the Zodiacal Animals incompatible with each. The elements of these incompatible animals according to the Twenty-Eight Constellations could be noted as in Table 2.3. It could be seen that the elements of the incompatible are often similar. That is, animals of similar element tend to be incompatible.

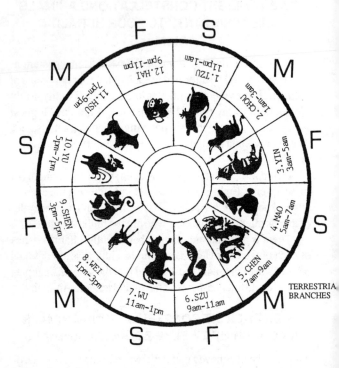

Figure 21.1: Incompatible Zodiac Animals.
Animals opposite each other are incompatible. Other animals incompatible are Rabbit:Tiger, Dragon:Cow, Snake:Rat, Horse: Pig, Goat:Dog and Monkey:Cock.
M = Metal; F = Fire; S = Sun.
Incompatible animals often have similar element sign.

Although the Zodiacal Animals are possible a modification of the Twenty-Eight Constellations, this relationship is incomplete. This is because the twenty-eight *hsiu* are of the Heavenly influences while the Twelve Zodiacal Animals represent the influences on Earth.

In a previous chapter we noted that the Dato spirit of the island of Pulau Tikus in Penang, Malaysia, is only one of the seven lieutenants (Ong, 1989, [personal commentary]). These lieutenants are under a General Spirit who ruled over the Malayan Main Range that stretched from southern Thailand. Chances are this General Spirit is under the East Angel of the Lord.

It would seem that going down the hierarchy we may have divisions based on seven's. That is, under each of the initial Four Heraldic Animals there would be seven assistants. Under each of these assistants there may be another seven lower assistants and so on.

The animals of the Twenty-Eight Constellations are also representations of the powers of Heaven as extensions of the Four Heraldic Animals. These *hsius* represent times when the geomancer would regard as most optimal to call on Heavenly powers to exert certain measures – something akin to the auspiciousness given to the new and full moon periods, believed to have influences on tidal movements. In fact, Table 2.3 shows that auspiciousness or inauspiciousness would be attached to each *hsiu* and this may reflect the availability or non-availability of the beneficent or maleficent aspects of the ruling angel.

The significance of the animals of Twenty-Eight Constellations to Chinese Animal Symbolism in general are only ill-understood at present and require further research studies.

22

CROCODILE

Link with: Earth *Lung*

HISTORICAL BACKGROUND

The Crocodile, or rather the Alligator, is a natural amphibious animal along the banks of the Yangtze River. It appears with the rainy season and the roll of thunder and then goes into hibernation until the following spring. This similarity of certain aspects of the habits of *Lung* have led a number of people to speculate that the Crocodile was the original animal on which the *Lung* was based on.

During the Tang times, the Crocodile lived at Ch'ao-chou where they were driven away by Han Yu and his officials with magic. They also occurred in Kuangsu where they were called *hu-lei* "sudden thunder" (Eberhard, 1968, p.365).

The Yangtze Alligator is depicted along with the *Lung* on a Shang bronze wine mixer (Figure 5.3). However, Williams (1931, pp.109-110) notes:

> The crocodile was worshipped by the ancient Egyptians, and one theory is that the Chinese *Lung* is a form of the alligator found occasionally in Yangtze River, for the emergence of the latter from hibernation synchronizes with the coming of spring, the time of *Lung*'s beneficent influence. However, it is difficult to trace this fabulous animal to any natural species, for the body of this *Lung* seems serpentine, its head with parts of various other animals, the teeth are those of a mammalian carnivore, while the legs and claws are those of a bird. Also, as it is a beneficent being, it cannot be compared with the ferocious dragon of heraldry

and mediaeval mythology. The dragon appears to perpetuate the tradition of primaeval flying saurians of geologic times, known only through their fossilized remains. The Lamas and Chinese Buddhists have assimilated them with the Indian mythical serpents (Naga).

The Crocodile is also mentioned in connection with an animal called *t' o* whose skin is used exclusively for the drumskin. This *t' o* is also linked with the chiao dragon, the Tortoise and with them are said to be connected with thunder (Eberhard, 1968, pp.364-365).

AUSPICIOUS MEANINGS OF CROCODILE

Despite the fact that the Crocodile is unlikely to be the *Lung* in the Twenty-Eight Constellations system it has been called the Earth *Lung*. The Earth *Lung* is linked with Chiao the Horn, four stars Spica, Zeta, Theta and Iota in the skirt of Virgo. The *Tong-Shu* describes is falling on a Thursday under the planet Jupiter. It is auspicious:

> To whomsoever builds on this day, this constellation will bring glory and prosperity, and men of letters will be able to approach near to the throne of the Emperor. Marriages on this day will result in numerous posterity. But to repair a tomb or go to a funeral may provoke a new grief.

It is said that in matters of dispute, the suspects would be placed before the Crocodile which is supposed to eat only the guilty one.

23

BADGER

HISTORICAL BACKGROUND

Snakes, Badgers, Weasels, small Deer and Hedgehogs are considered to be the Five Seers and have to be treated with reverence and the respect which increase with their age. They usually take up their homes in old and dilapidated buildings and if they are not well treated, unpleasantness will follow. If anyone is made ill by one of the animals, it is difficult to find exorcist to deal with some of them; for the exorcism is very specialized and the specialist for one animal may not be able to deal with another.

AUSPICIOUS MEANING OF BADGER

The Five Seers or *Wu Sheng* are also depended on to keep diseases off from farmers' poultry yards and pigsties.

It is third lunar constellation, *Ti*, meaning bottom or root, composing of four stars in the design of a measure, Alpha, Beta, Gamma and Iota in Libra's bottom. The *Tong-Shu* describes that it falls on a Saturday under the planet Saturn and is inauspicious:

> To build on this day will be inauspicious enough, and the celebration of marriages will bring endless calamities. Journey by boat will be shipwrecked. Funerals will cause the impoverishment of descendants.

24

THE FOX

HISTORICAL BACKGROUND

The Fox (Figure 24.1) is a well-known animal in Chinese mythology, They are many stories which concern Fox fairies. The Fox is endowed with high supernatural qualities.

Foxes were at times seen coming out of old coffins or graves and hence regarded as souls of the dead. Living in caves and holes, the Fox is said to be near the *Yin* or female forces of the underworld. Its home is neither earth of life or Hades of death – but the Fox acquires supernatural energy as a result. His dwelling is among the tombs and the spirits of the dead often possess the body of the Fox. Thus, it enables ghosts to return to life or himself performs their terrible wishes including those of revenge, thereby bringing peace to souls who otherwise would be travellingforever with a troubled mind.

The Fox is also one of the creatures the souls of dead would ride on their way to the nether world.

Chinese philosophers said that the Fox could live a long life of eight hundred years and even up to a thousand years. This long life is supposed to be due to the Fox living in caves and holes free from disturbance and the wearing effects of light and heat. It is claimed that in ancient times when men lived in caves they too had long life as evident from their generally larger sizes.

The Fox spirit would take human form only at nights. The Fox is said to be able to assume human forms more thoroughly in the Peking area than elsewhere in the empire. The Fox appears most frequently as a pretty girl to do mischief. The disguised woman is always young and beautiful, generally wicked but occasionally good. It could put on the garb and appearance of someone familiar either dead or living at a great distance (Dennys, 1968, p.94).

Figure 24.1: The Fox.
Fox spirits are well-known in Chinese folklores. The Fox symbolizes longevity and craftiness.

The Fox is regarded as a cunning and crafty animal able to disarm the suspicions of its prey. The Fox's intelligence is said to be seen when it crosses a frozen river very slowly and deliberately, putting his head close to the ice to listen to the running waters. A traveller could thus use the Fox footsteps across the ice and snow as a safe path.

AUSPICIOUS MEANINGS OF FOX

The Chinese regard the Fox as an emblem of longevity and craftiness. Some people may worship it to obtain wealth. Mandarins of old used to put their documents in "Fox chambers" which do not have the word "Fox" to avoid irritating it. Instead another word which sounds like "Fox" is used to gain its assistance to look after the documents. If a document was lost one could invoke the Fox to help get it back.

Fox spirits are among the Five Feared Animals, the equivalent of western werewolves. But where the western werewolves are usually evil and fearsome, Fox spirits are either beneficent or maleficent depending on the circumstances.

It is said that at the age of fifty the Fox could assume the form of a woman, and that at one hundred it could become a young and beautiful girl or a wizard with great magical powers. After one thousand years old he enters heaven to become a celestial Fox (Denny, 1968).

The Fox represents the fifth lunar constellation of *Hsin* the Heart, three stars in Scorpio. The *Tong-Shu* describes that the day of this fifth constellation is a Monday, under the Moon, and is inauspicious:

> To build today will be most inauspicious and everything will lead to ruin, sooner or later. Similarly burials and marriages will be seen to be disastrous and will assure three years of repeated calamities

AUSPICIOUS LEGENDS OF FOX

There are several tales about the Fox in the Chinese literature. The most famous Fox tale must be that of Ta Chi, the mistress of Chou Hsin, the last emperor of the Shang dynasty.

TA CHI OF THE SHANG DYNASTY

As Emperor Chou Hsin angered the Goddess Nu Hua in a visit to her temple, the Goddess sent three spirits – a thousand years Fox spirit, a three-headed pheasant spirit and a jade *pipa* spirit – to destroy the Shang dynasty. Ta Chi, the daughter of Marquis Su Hu was possessed by the Fox spirit on her way to be given to Emperor Chou Hsin. After sometime, Ta Chi began to spoil the emperor, made him neglect the affairs of the empire and goaded him to commit excesses against his officials. A number of holy men tried to exorcize the evil spirit but Ta Chi was able to trick the emperor against them. Ta Chi was credited with the invention of the torture where the victim would be humiliated by being stripped naked and then chained against a hollow metal cylinder in which a fire was set up – the helpless victim would scream as the heat became unbearable and his body would eventually be roasted alive and turned into charred black mass. Ta Chi also brought other Fox spirits into the palace. However, these were involved in a feast and were drunk. Pi-Kan, the Prime Minister followed them to their Fox-den and ordered a general to burn the den and kill the Foxes. For this Ta Chi instigated the Emperor against Pi-Kan who had to perform auto-surgery to take out his own spleen for the Emperor. One by one the loyal and able men either abandoned or were driven from the emperor – most of them eventually went to the side of King Wen of Chou state which eventually overcame the Shang. The mistress Ta Chi played a prominent role in the downfall and the Fox Spirit which possessed her was blamed.

Table 24.1

Fox Sayings

Sayings about the Fox normally reflect the basic bewitching nature of the Fox:

- Fox spirit loves fruit not jewellry: Used against accusation that the fox spirit stole the items.
- Fox has a bewitching pearl: Can bewitch people.
- The Fox spirit can change into a man but cannot change its tail: Blood will tell.
- The Fox tail is out: The secret is out.
- Transformed from a Fox: treacherous.
- Fox walking as a Tiger: Taking advantage of power to perform evil.
- Do not incite the nine-tail fox: Not safe to provoke.
- Talk of the devil and he comes, talk of the fox and its tail is shown.
- Wolves block the road why look at foxes?: The great robber is at large why bother petty thieves?
- Burn off a Fox's tail: One promoted to higher office or received a literary degree.

THE LEOPARD

HISTORICAL BACKGROUND

The Leopard is classed as one of the four animals, along with the Elephant, Tiger and Lion, representing power.

AUSPICIOUS MEANINGS OF LEOPARD

It is an emblem of bravery and martial ferocity. It is the animal embroidered onto robes of military officials of the third grade.

The Leopard's (and at times Tiger's) tail is also associated with Hsi Wang-Mu, the famous Queen Mother of the West (see chapter on Tiger).

It is the seventh lunar constellation, the Basket. The *Tong-Shu* describes that it falls on a Wednesday, under the planet Mercury and is auspicious:

> To build today leads to assurance of power and the beginning of any venture will give the family greater good fortune. Repairing of burial places and marriages will be good; coffers will overflow with silver and gold and the storehouses with grains of all kinds.

THE BAT

HISTORICAL BACKGROUND

*P*ien fu refers to the family of Bats (Figure 26.1). *Fu-i*, "covering wings", refers to the widespread wings as the Bat flies about. It is also symbolically linked to the Rat and Swallow as evidenced in its other nicknames *t'ien shu* (Heaven Rat), *hsien shu* (Sagecous Rat), *fei shu* (Flying Rat) and *yeh yen* (Night Swallow).

Figure 26.1: The Bat.
Auspicious symbol of good fortune, happiness and longevity.

The *Pen Ts' ao* (Chinese Herbal) refers to a Bat species in the caverns of the hills that may live up to a thousand years and become white as silver. Eating this Bat was believed to give long life and good eyesight. The eyesight legend is based on the apparently unerring ability of the Bat in avoiding obstacles during its swift flight. This is not due to the eyesight as the Bat is virtually blind but attributed to the sophisticated radar system associated with its ears.

The Bat is one of the most common luck motifs used in many ornamental forms so much so that many forms look very much like the Butterfly. It is commonly associated with the Phoenix or Dragon in diagrams of auspicious symbols.

AUSPICIOUSNESS

Although in the West, the Bats are associated with the dark forces, but the Chinese regard them as omens of good fortune. A very auspicious good luck motif is the five or four Bats surrounding the Shou character; "Shou" means longevity which is quite popular as images on "red packet" for the New Year. The symbol represents the Five Fortunes of old age, wealth, health, love of virtue and a natural death.

The Chinese character for Bat is *fuk shu* which means Rat of Happiness. If the Bat rushes into the house it is a sign that good luck is coming to the occupant.

The Bat is the emblem of happiness and longevity. It would be painted red, the colour of joy.

In funerals, lanterns and other paper pieces with Bat images are also seen; they are actually good wishes symbols; asking the dead souls to bless their family.

The curved wing of the Bat was often carved onto the short sword known as the *Joo-I* – anciently used for self-defence and gesticulation. It was also presented as good wishes for prosperity. Its shape is said to derive from the sacred fungus which is the plant of long life. The head of the

Joo-I is where the most ornate carvings are made and bear a strong resemblance to the Bat of good omen with the pomegranate, a fruit of another good augury. The *Joo-I* is given to male infants while the female normally would receive a concave tile (Williams, 1931, p.205). This *Joo-I* could be akin to the Malay keris, although it has be said to be the equivalent to the Buddhist Diamond Mace.

ASTROLOGICAL SIGNIFICANCE

The Bat represents the tenth of the twenty-eight constellations, namely, *Nu* the Girl, which have four stars in the shape of a sieve in the left hand of Aquarius. The *Tong-Shu* describes that it falls on a Saturday under the planet Saturn and is inauspicious:

> To build today will be very damaging to the charm of pretty women and make brothers quarrel among themselves like tigers and wolves. Marriages and burials will cause luck to disappear and cause the family to migrate.

Chang Kou-Lau, one of the Eight Immortals, and the one with the lute and riding the Donkey backward, is also claimed to be the incarnation of the "White Bat" from the "First or Primeval Chaos" (Burkhardt, 1982, pp.163,166).

THE SWALLOWS

HISTORICAL BACKGROUND

The Chinese character for Swallow is a pictogram showing its head, body, wings and tail. The commonest Swallow is *Hirundo gutturalis* in central and northern China. The Striped Swallow, *H. nipolensis* and the Reed Swallow are also found. But the famous bird's nest is made from the gelatinous nests of the Sea Swallow, *H. esculenta* which stays in caves. Peking is also known as the City of Swallow on account of the numerous birds.

The Swallow (Figure 27.1) is said to hate the sacred plant Artemesia, owing to the strong fragrance of the plant (Eberhard, 1968, p.156).

Some have tried to interpret the Swallow as the actual Phoenix (Eberhard, 1968, p.430).

AUSPICIOUS MEANINGS OF SWALLOW

The spring equinox is connected with the Swallows' return. A flight of Swallows is an especially good omen for the Chinese. The Chinese would never deliberately kill the Swallow (Dennys, 1968, p.34). The coming of Swallows and their nesting in new places would be hailed as signs of success and prosperity to the occupiers of the premises.

Swallows are also drawn in Chinese paintings in pairs among the willow tree and have the same significance as a pair of Ducks among lotus in symbolizing marital harmony. This wise, the Swallow also symbolizes the coming of spring.

Women's voices are compared to twittering of Swallows while the bird's nest is applied to weak position.

Figure 27.1: The Swallow.
A flight of swallows is a good omen, signalling success, prosperity
and even martial harmony. The Swallow is also regarded as the
ancestral emblem of the Shang Dynasty.

The Swallow represents the twelfth lunar constellation of Wei, Danger or the Roof, the three stars as an obtuse triangle in the left shoulder of Aquarius. The *Tong-Shu* describes it falling on a Monday under the planet Moon and as inauspicious:

Nothing large should be built this day and burial or tombs repairs will induce blood flow. Do not open a business or irrigate the paddy fields, as these will bring unhappiness and trouble at courts.

The *Lung* is said to eat the Swallow. When people pray to the *Lung* for rains they may sacrifice Swallows (Williams, 1931, p.110).

AUSPICIOUS LEGENDS OF SWALLOW

Shang rulers regarded themselves as descendants of the Swallow. Princess Keen-Tieh of the House of Sung, married Emperor K'uh of the Shang dynasty and went with him in the vernal equinox sacrifice when the Swallow made its first appearance. The Swallow laid an egg which the princess ate. Seeh her son was thus said to be born from a mystic union with the Swallow. It is sang (Waterbury, 1952, p.84):

Heaven commissioned the Swallow
To descend and give birth to Shang (Odes of Sung).

PORCUPINE

HISTORICAL BACKGROUND

Like Snakes, Badgers, Weasels, and small Deer, Porcupines (Hedgehogs) are considered to be the Five Seers and have to be treated with reverence and the respect increases with their age. The Five Seers or *Wu Sheng* are also depended on to keep diseases off the farmers' poultry yards and pigsties They take up their homes in old and dilapidated buildings and if not well-treated, unpleasantness will follow. If anyone is made ill by one of the animals, it is difficult to find an exorcist to deal with some of them because a specialist for one animal may not be able to deal with another.

The Hedgehog or Porcupine is one of the five calamity animals with the Fox, Weasel, Snake and Rat. The proverb "Like running against the claws of the five animals" refers to these five animals which could cause turbulent insanity and great disturbances. They are greatly feared and worshipped as the Five Great Families. Their particular habit of lying down on the way often cause people to step on their claws and thus attacked.

It is interesting to note that the Porcupine was also found in the combination of the poisonous animals the Frog and Scorpion in ancient Sumerian pottery (Waterbury, 1952, p.21)

AUSPICIOUS MEANINGS OF PORCUPINE

The Porcupine is the fourteenth lunar constellation, Pi the Wall, composing of two stars, Gamma or Algenib in the wing tip of Pegasus and Alpha of the head of Andromeda. The

Tong-Shu describes that it falls on a Wednesday under the planet Mercury. It is auspicious:

> To build today will bring great fortunes; marriages will bring peace and joy. Funerals will ensure wealth and prosperous progenies. To begin an enterprise or to water a paddy field will assure descendants.

THE WOLF

HISTORICAL BACKGROUND

The Wolf is very common in China and does a great deal of harm in the sheep-fold and farmyard. White rings are painted on the walls in the belief that the Wolf on seeing these rings would flee from the supposed traps.

The three species of the Chow dogs in China are believed to descend from the Wolf. These are fierce large one-man dogs, suspicious of all except the master (Burkhardt, 1982, p.193).

The Unicorn is said to possess the forehead of a Wolf (Burkhardt, 1982, p.178).

AUSPICIOUS MEANINGS OF WOLF

The Wolf is a symbol of cupidity and rapaciousness. It represents the official who extracts money unfairly from the people especially in the shape of unauthorized taxations.

The evil Wolf spirit is almost as feared as the evil Tiger spirit. It would prey on common pathways of men and kill the unwary traveller. It could change form to lure the victim. Dogs were often used to hunt them out and kill these Wolves.

Unlike the Tiger or Fox, which may have both evil and good forms, the Wolf seems entirely evil. Sayings about the Wolf show its evil treacherous nature:

> Everywhere in the world, the Wolf will eat men; while the Dog will eat refuse: One able will have plenty while the person of little ability is always in need.

> Tiger heart and Wolf face: Smiling and treacherous.

Wolf and Pei are treacherous: Two evil persons cooperating to do wickedness

Beat a Wolf with a sharp stalk – both parties afraid: The aggressor fears as he knows his weakness, but one on defence fear being unaware of the other's weakness

Tiger in front Wolf at back: Dilemma

The Wolf represents the fifteenth lunar constellation Kuei the Astride, sixteen stars in Pisces. The day of this constellation falls on a Thursday under the planet Jupiter. It is inauspicious:

To build today will be very auspicious. Harmony and Prosperity will blow through the door of the family home. But a burial today will produce mysterious death, and to do business or flood a paddy field will only attract calamity.

THE PHEASANT

HISTORICAL BACKGROUND

Most common of the Chinese Pheasants is the Ring-Necked Pheasant, *Phasianus torquatus*, found everywhere. The Golden Pheasant, *P. pictus*, is found in the south. the Silver Pheasant, *P. nycthemerus* is in Fukien and Chekiang. Reeve's Pheasant is found in the north mountains. The mythical Phoenix may be a form of the Argus Pheasant or Peacock.

There is a belief that in the fall and winter, Pheasants and Sparrows enter into the water to become mussels (Eberhard, 1968, p.291).

The Pheasant is known as early as the Shang times, where it was depicted as the evil Pheasant spirit, whom the Goddess Nu Kua sent, with two other spirits, to the last Shang Emperor, the tyrant Chou Tsin. One of the other two evil spirits is the famous Ta Chi, the Fox spirit with nine tails.

AUSPICIOUS MEANINGS OF PHEASANT

The Golden Pheasant was embroidered on robes of court officials of the second grade while the Silver Pheasant on those of the fifth grade. The bird is shown standing on a rock in the sea looking at the sun, the Imperial symbol of authority.

The bird is depicted as a symbol of courage and an animal of the sun and also of thunder.

The Pheasant is one of the eight animals represented by the Eight Diagrams, being the equivalent of Li, Fire; which incidentally is also the emblem of the Phoenix (Burkhardt, 1982, p.112).

The Pheasant represents the seventeenth lunar constellation Wei the Stomach, three main stars in Musca Borealis. The *Tong-Shu* describes it as falling on a Saturday, under the planet Saturn and as being auspicious:

> To those who build today all comes like a wind blowing precious glory and fortunes and many joys. Marriages will be of flourishing harmony and funerals will bring social promotion.

THE CROW also RAVEN

HISTORICAL BACKGROUND

The Crow or Raven features in many ancient cultures. The Black Crow, *Corvus macrorhynchus* and its white collar relative *C. torquatus* are common in China. They have raucous voices.

The Crow is differentiated from the Magpie by the fact that the Magpie has a white underbelly. However, in some legends, they are inter-equivalent.

AUSPICIOUS MEANINGS OF CROW

The Golden Crow (Figure 46.1), which has a golden collar, is the symbol of the sun and is also a symbol of filial piety as it is said to take care of its parents when disabled or old and to disgorge food for their sustenance. In fact in the Bible these Crows brought food to sustain the prophet Elijah in the wilderness! The Raven that was sacred during the Chou times was the sacred emblem of the sun and was known as the Sun Raven (Eberhard, 1968, p.429) which is likely the Golden Crow.

The Raven is associated with Emperor Shun and is supposed to bring earth to the grave of those who were filial (Eberhard, 1968, p.267).

However, the Chinese dislikes the Black Crow, especially the white-winged Raven, as it is an omen of evil:

> Crow, crow get out of my sight,
> Or else I'll eat thy liver and light.

The cry of the Crow is especially inauspicious and hearing it should make a person postpones action on any important affair. The Crow crying out near the house when a person is sick is also considered a very bad sign. The Chinese would mutter invocation against the evil harbinger. Its voice "Ka! Ka!" sounds like "Bite! Bite!" in Chinese and a term that is not so lucky, unless it is cawing between 3 to 7 am from the south. Between 7 to 11 am it portends wind and rain.

When Crows gather in corners of a city they indicates possibilities of impending drought and infighting. Should they gather on the roof of a house that drought is imminent. Crows gathering in a house means sorrow. Seating on one's head would bring poverty to the man and on a lady's head her husband is in deep trouble. People whose heads are sat on by crows should offer sesame oil and clothing to the poor or deserving persons.

ASTROLOGICAL SIGNIFICANCE

The Raven represents the nineteenth lunar constellation, Pi the End, of the Thread, six stars in Hades and Nim and Nun in Taurus. It falls on a Monday under the influence of the Moon. The Crow is also associated with the third Moon as denoting the end of spring. the *Tong-Shu* describes it as auspicious:

> There will be light on those who build. Paddy growing and silkworm rearing will have years of plenty. Luck and fortune will come to your home. Funerals and marriages will bring doubled longevity.

AUSPICIOUS LEGENDS OF CROW

The Crow, or rather the three-legged Sun Raven or Golden Crow, features in the legend of Feng-I (husband of Chang-O the Moon Goddess) shooting at the ten suns. During the time of Emperor Yao, the ten suns were supposed to take turns one by one in patrolling the sky. But the ten suns suddenly appeared in the sky. The climate became very hot and the land and crops dried up.

There was no water and people suffered. So Emperor Yao ordered the Divine Archer Feng-I to deal with the problem. Feng-I shot down nine of the suns, which happened to be nine three-legged black crows. The remaining sun was spared and since then this sun had to patrol the sky forever.

The inauspicious nature of the Crow is reflected in a fable about them and the Owls.

THE CROWS AND THE OWL

There was once a group of Crows living in close proximity with another group of Owls. The Crows sleep at night and the Owls at day. They attacked each other and the slaughter was great. Then an intelligent Crow said this could not go on and thought up a plan to exterminate the Owls so that they could live in peace. This Crow asked his companions to attack him, peck at him and pull out a number of his feathers. So, in sorry state he went to the Owls and complained of his bad treatment. One of the Owls pitying him took him in. When his feathers had grown, this Crow set out and built a pile of brushwood around the Owls' hole. He pretended to explain that in return for the Owls' kindness he was building a shield against the cold winds. During a snowstorm the Owls crowded into the hole. The Crow seizing his opportunity plucked a fire from nearby and placed it into the brushwood. The Owls were smothered to death (Dennys, 1968, p.150).

Moral: Never trust a renegade

THE TAPIR

The Tapir is a large Pig-like animal with a half black half white body. It belongs to the same family as the Rhinoceros, Hippopotamus and Ox.

This Tapir is the twenty-second Constellation, Ching the Well, composing of eight stars, four in the feet and four in the knees in Gemini. The *Tong-Shu* describes it falling on a Thursday under the planet Jupiter and as auspicious:

> To build today would lead to prosperity in paddy fields and silkworm rearing. The family would be first among the golden list. Every venture would bring success and wealth and many inheritors. Take care in funerals where the dead dies a violent death.

It is difficult to trace any other real significance attached to the Tapir which is a rather strange beast for the ancient Chinese to note. Either the animal was more common in ancient times or the animal may be actually a reference to better known animal like the Rhinoceros or Water-Buffaloes.

THE DEER (BUCK)

Also 26th Constellation (STAG).

HISTORICAL BACKGROUND

The Hog-Deer, antelopes abound in China while the yak, a form of Deer, is found in Tibet. The Deer was a common catch of the Shang hunter. They frequent water areas not far from human settlements thus living close to man. One reason why the animal was hunted was that large groups of Deer often damage crops. The skin, antlers and meat of the animal are very useful to man (Hsu and Ward, 1984, p.50).

The Unicorn is said to resemble a large Stag, with the body of a musk Deer, tail of an Ox, forehead of a Wolf and Horses' hooves.

The Stag is credited with a life span of a thousand years before its skin turns grey and then in another five hundred years its skin would be white (Burkhardt, 1982, p.208). Hunters sometimes sacrifice the Stag to the Mountain God.

AUSPICIOUS MEANINGS OF DEER

The Deer is believed to live long and is therefore an emblem of long life (Figure 33.1). It is often depicted as the mount of the God of Longevity (the Star God Canopus in the constellation of Argo) and the large peach. The peach is the *P'an Tao*, found only in the Kun Lun Mountains, which flowers every three thousand years and the fruits mature three thousand years later. Deer's horns are made into various products. People eat hawthorns at great costs trying to prolong their life.

It is said to be the only animal able to find the Ling-Chi, the Fungus of Immortality. The Deer, after a mating, is said to search for the ginseng roots. Thus, following a mating Deer could lead a person to a ginseng groove.

The Deer is also an emblem of official emolument as the Chinese character has a similar pronunciation.

The Indian said that it is auspicious to see Deer on the right side of the road, or groups of three or fives. But it is bad to see a lone black Deer.

Figure 33.1: The Deer.
An emblem of long life. Often associated with the Peach and the God of Longevity.

Like Snakes, Badgers, Weasels, and Hedgehogs, small Deer are considered to be the Five Seers and have to be treated with reverence and the respect increases with their age.

ASTROLOGICAL SIGNIFICANCE

The Deer is the twenty-fourth and the Stag is twenty-sixth constellations, Liu the Willow and Chang, Drawing a Bow or Fishing Net, falling on Saturday ruled by the planet Saturn and Monday ruled by the planet Moon. Liu composes of eight stars in one coil of Hydra while Chang composes of five stars in another coil of Hydra. The *Tong-Shu* describes the twenty-fourth constellation as inauspicious but the twenty-sixth constellation as auspicious:

Twenty-fourth constellation: To build today lead to legal troubles; thieves and disasters will endanger the house. Funerals and marriages will be followed by series of miseries

Twenty-sixth constellation: A pavilion built on this day will enable descendant of officials to approach the Emperor. Flooding the paddy field and funerals will attract money and riches. Marriages will be of unending harmony and happiness.

AUSPICIOUS LEGEND ABOUT DEER

Besides the God of Longevity, the Deer is also associated with the Crab with Li Tieh-Kuai, the Beggar Immortal of the Eight Immortals.

There is a fable of the Tiger which was about to eat the Monkey. But the Monkey told the Tiger he was too small a meal for the great Tiger and that he would lead the Tiger to a better meal. The Monkey brought the Tiger to a Stag. However, the Stag, realizing the situation, cried out to the Monkey: "How come that you brought only one tiger when you have promised me ten tiger skins." On hearing this the Tiger was alarmed, it ran off, vowing never to trust the treacherous Monkey again. (Dennys, 1968, p.148)

THE SILKWORM

Silk is a highly valued cloth material in China, Japan and throughout the world. It is spun by the Silkworms which feed on mulberry leaves. The art of rearing Silkworms and spinning silk yarn have been known from ancient times, being attributed to the Lady Hsi-Ling, the Consort of Huang-Ti the Yellow Emperor (2695BC). China was the first nation to produce and utilise silk, followed by Japan and others.

There are actually a number of varieties of Silkworms such as *Bombax mori* producing the white silk, *Tussah* or *Antheraea mylitta* producing brown silk.

Silkworms are believed to belong to the *Yang* or male principle and under the protection of a certain constellation. Any male things like the sun, men, etc. is considered congenial to the Silkworms. But ladies, especially pregnant ladies are deleterious to Silkworms and its industry. Even the presence of a new-born child is considered not good for the Worm (Dennys, 1968, pp.70-71)

The Silkworm is thus a sign of industry and its product of delicate purity and virtue (Williams, 1931, p.325)

The Silkworm festival is on the third Day of the third Moon. Amulets are worn to promote silk production. On this festival girls involved with the trade should be touched by strangers (Eberhard, 1968, pp.34-35).

During the fifth Day of the fifth Moon, the *Ku* charm would be prepared. It is usually a love and wealth charm but could also be used to harm others. The more people get killed the richer the *Ku* owner becomes. The dead victims are said to become slaves to the owner of the *Ku* and could have intercourse with human beings. The souls are called "gold Silkworms" (Eberhardt, 1968, pp.150-151).

Silk of five colours are used to make amulets as protection against war and appear to be takeovers of previous flowers charms (Eberhard, 1968, p.157).

Earthworms which copulate on the fifth Day of the fifth Moon are supposed to make love charms in south China. Some people, like the way they eat Frogs, likes to eat these Earthworms in dried form (Eberhard, 1968, p.146).

Worms are connected with the twenty-eighth and last constellation Chen, the Cross-bar of the Chariot, composing of four stars Beta, Gamma, Delta, Epsilon in Corvus. The *Tong-Shu* describes it as falling on a Wednesday under the planet Mercury and being auspicious:

> To build this day would bring promotion. Marriages would receive the Emperor's blessing. Funerals will brighten the star of the lettered person. Prosperity would be equal to a cart of gold and a mountain of jade.

MISCELLANEOUS ANIMALS: INTRODUCTION

About twenty-nine different animals, including the Bat and five different birds compose the significance of the animal symbolism in the Ganzhi System, namely:

Four Heraldic Animals	– 7 animals
Zodiac Animals	– 12 (with 3 in the Heraldic Animals)
Twenty-Eight Constellations	– 28 (with 14 in the Zodiac Animals)

It should be emphasized again that the ancient records indicate that these animal symbolism fundamentally reflect the images of angelic spirits of very high order; of the high classes of cherubims and seraphims. The ancient Chinese records also regard them as messenger spirits from God. Their spheres of influences and hierarchy, whether in heaven or on earth or both and at particular periods of time, appear to be defined by the Ganzhi System.

However, this book further shows that significant parts of the animal symbolism are also anthropomorphic development of legends of famous ancient Chinese figures. It is possible that further analysis of these anthropomorphic animal symbolism could reveal some interesting points about ancient Chinese history.

There is still a wide range of other miscellaneous animals. This section describes the significance of these other animals, such as the Cat, Donkey, Elephant, Lion, Rhinoceros, Squirrel; watery creatures like Fish, Oysters and Mussels, Prawn; the five Poisonous Animals, a range of Insects and Birds.

These animals are not directly linked to the Ganzhi system. As the descriptions will indicate, most of these other animals are linked to one or the other of the animals of the

Ganzhi system and have overlapping significance with these other animals. For example, the five Poisonous Animals (Snake, Centipede, Scorpion or Spider, Lizard, Toad) seem to be a negation of the positive Four plus One Heraldic Animals.

In the ultimate analysis, the Chinese animal symbolism, which covers over seventy different animals (including birds and insects), are all connected to the Ganzhi System.

Remember again: Man is superior to all these animals.

36

THE CAT

Linked with: Hare (Cat = wild Hare) Tiger,
Fox (Cat = domestic Fox)

HISTORICAL BACKGROUND

Although Cats are very common household animals in China (Figure 36.1), it has been noted that it is not one of the Twelve Zodiac Animals of the Twelve Terrestrial Branches, neither was it significant in the Twenty-Eight Constellations. This could be because the Cat was not indigenous in China. However, the Cat was mentioned by the Book of Odes and so was already in China since ancient times.

But the wild Cat has been a replacement for the Rabbit in North China as the word "Rabbit" is an insult. In Vietnam, the astrological Rabbit is said to be replaced by the Cat (De Kermadec and Poulson, 1983, p.32).

The ancient Chinese character for Cat is that of an animal catching rats in the rice field. The earliest records of Cats are from Egypt, which was then the granary of the civilized world (Burkhardt, 1982, p.194).

Like the Dog, the Cat, is not regarded as a pet, for the Chinese use them for utility purposes and normally tie them with chains and leashes. Among the poorer classes and the Cantonese, Cats are sometimes fatten for food.

It is said that the Cat's eye is able to tell the time. At midnight, noon, sunrise and sunset the Cat's eye is like a thread. At 4 and 10 o'clock morning and evening it is like the full moon. At 2 and 8 o'clock it is elliptical. The Cat's nose is always cold except at the Summer Solstice when it is warm (Burkhardt, 1982, p.195).

The Hare is also called a wild or hill Cat, *Shan Mao*. The Cat is affiliated with the Tiger and is also called the domestic Fox.

Figure 36.1: The Cat.
Protector of Silkworms. However, generally the Cat is usually regarded as an evil creature. It is the one animal who missed being included in the Twelve Zodiac Animals.

AUSPICIOUS MEANINGS OF CAT

The Cat is well-known for catching the rats which come to get the grains. Rats destroy silkworm and Cats are used to keep them away and because of this the Cats are regarded as the patron saint of the Silkworms.

The Butterfly Cat, whose skin has blotched not striped markings, is considered lucky. Kitten of certain golden shade is welcome as it is the Money Cat which will bring financial blessings. Cat and Butterfly are often combined to convey the wishes for 80 to 90 years of life (Figure 36.2). The wishes are based on puns of the words. Butterfly (Tieh) is for 70 to 80; while Cat (Mao) is for 80 to 90. They also form favourite images on jade.

The Cat, through their affinity with the Tiger, is said to be able to scare off evil spirits. Just as Dogs chase away human marauders, the Cats chase away spirits.

Chang Hsien, the guardian of children, who shoots at the Sky Rat, is surrounded by a brace of red Cats, each with two tails. (q.v. Rat).

In China the Cat is also regarded to be in league with the dark forces and include meteorological prescience. It is also known as the domestic Fox. Owing to this the Cat is sometimes used as a popular charm. It may be placed on the roofs as a clay pussy with a bob-tail to ward off evil influences. The evil repute of the Cat among the Chinese seems to parallel the western fear of Cats as the animals of witches. One tale illustrates its demonic attributes (Dennys, 1968, p.91).

In Leong Chow, the people do homage to a Cat ghost in the province of Kansuh and in the history of the North. They begin this by first hanging the Cat, and then perform ceremonies of fasting and requiems for seven weeks to establish the spiritual communication. The spirit is then transferred to a wooden tablet and put up behind the door where the Cat is honoured with offerings. By the side of it is a bag of about five inches long and this is for the Cat's use. From time to time it steals people's things and about the fourth watch of the night before the cock crows the bag disappears. It will be found hanged up on the corner of the house, and a ladder is used to fetch it down. When the bag is opened and inverted, as much as two hundred catties of rice or peas will be in it. Those who serve it become rich very fast.

Cats are inauspicious animals. If a cat follows a person home and stay it foreshadows poverty and distress. The converse is true if it is a dog. The Cat's visit seems to link to the rats being able to thrive when the house is dilapidated. It is unlucky when a Cat is stolen from a house. If a pregnant female cat walks over the dead, the dead will rise up and pursue those nearest to it and strangle anyone it catches.

There is an obscure Egyptian connection between the Cat and the sun. Bastet, the sun-goddess had a Cat head and represented the sun's beneficent powers while Sekhovet with the head of a lioness represented the sun's destructive powers (Whitticks, 1960, p.157)

The Indians have a number of Cat omens (Biljawan, 1977). When a person starts on a journey, the mewing Cat with food in its mouth is a good sign but not if it has no food. If a person who is on a journey sees a Cat on the left side of the road it is good sign but not if the Cat crosses the road. It is bad if a Cat falls on a sleeping person. The Cat licking a woman is very bad – for if it licks the forehead her husband is in danger, her breast her son is in danger, her foot her father-in-law is in danger and could lead to death.

AUSPICIOUS LEGENDS OF CAT

A fable, undoubtedly of Buddhist origins, indicates the evil nature of the Cat (Dennys, 1968 p.147):

> Once a man playfully placed a rosary on the neck of a Cat. The mice saw the old Cat sitting mewing with half closed eyes. The mice were surprised and said: "Cat is reformed as she is praying. We do not have to fear her anymore." So they came near the Cat. The Cat suddenly sprang and killed several of them. The other mice fled and cried out "Who thought a Cat with closed eyes and reciting prayers would behave like that!" Others cried out: "We thought Cat was praying to Buddha, but his piety was false."

HOW THE CAT MISSED THE ZODIAC ROLL

See page 134 for the tale on how the cat missed being named as one of the Zodiac animals by Buddha.

The Cat waited for a revenge for being left out of the Zodiac roll call by the Rat and an opportunity arose when the Buddha died:

> When Sakyamuni Buddha was born he was able to stand up in the tub of water. Then the Buddha died. The Lord was laid down on the bier, an angelic smile on his face. He was surrounded by his disciples, the divas and spirits and even animals, all weeping. The Rat was going to visit Mayabunin the mother of Buddha, but not watchful in its grief, was pounced on by the Cat who tore it to pieces. Hence in the paintings of the moving scenes of Buddha's death, there is no Cat painted. According to legend the Cat daily approached on the great artist, the Japanese Cho Denso, and wept at being left out. The Cat was forever

mewing and grieving. Finally Cho Denso in pity painted the Cat into a picture of the Buddha's death. The Cat out of joy fell over dead. The picture is still preserved in the Temple To Fuku at Kyoto (Bowie, 1911, p.97).

THE DONKEY

The Donkey, like the Cat, is not part of the Twelve Zodiacal Animals nor is it among the Twenty-Eight Constellations. Hence, it is believed that the animal is not indigenous to China. They are eaten and also used for dry-ploughing.

However, the white Donkey is the animal ridden by the Immortal Chang Kou-Lao of the Eight Immortals who, holding a musical bamboo instrument, is usually shown riding the animal backwards. Sometimes he rides the Toad. The Immortal after riding the animal would fold it up like a paper slip and put it into his pocket!

The Donkey is a symbol of stupidity, just as it is to Westerners. The nature of the Donkey is reflected in the tale of the ass who was ambitious and wanted to be as strong as the Ox. So he first went about eating the food of the Ox. He went about mixing with the horned beasts. When he felt that everything was well he proceeded to change his usual braying and gave out the deep-toned moo of his horned companions. But the cattle were not amused. Angry at the insult they hemmed the ass in and gored him to death. (Dennys, 1968, p.148)

The Indian said that a journeying man seeing a Donkey on the left side of the road is good; if on the right side it is bad. The hooting of a Donkey whether behind or in front is inauspicious. Coupling Donkeys signifies success of work.

THE ELEPHANT

HISTORICAL BACKGROUND

Today, the Elephant is the largest land animal. It thrives in hot damp climates. It is a docile animal but one must be wary not to provoke it. The strength of the Elephant is believed to lies in its trunk which if injured would cause the death of the animal.

In China it was a rare animal before the Shang time (Hsu and Ward, 1984, p.46). The capture of Elephants was mentioned in the Shang oracle bones, and tombs of twenty-one Elephants were found in the Shang capital. In Chou times, the Elephant was extinct in Honan but was still found in Yangtze region. By Han times, it was already rare even in south China. In Sung times the animal could still be found in south China. Dancing Elephants were known as early as the Chou period. They were also used as war Elephants in 506BC by King Chao of Ch'u. Gigantic monuments of Elephants are found in the Ming tombs. The Elephant were also found in Yunan and before that further north in Kwangtung. The drift in the habitat of the Elephant in China could be said to indicate that the climate in ancient China became cooler from the Shang dynasty to the Han dynasty and the animal was forced to migrate southwards.

Ivory has been a popular Chinese material for ornaments and items of worship. Ivory was known in ancient China as far back as 6,000 years ago. The Chinese has a high demand for the ivory of the Elephant. They are carved into several types of beautiful ornamental objects. This leads to hunting of the animal which is another reason the animals were extinct in most areas of China.

In ancient terminology the several references to the river pig actually refers to the Elephant. The Elephant is said to be used for plowing by Emperor Shun (Eberhard, 1968, pp.258, 265).

AUSPICIOUS MEANINGS OF ELEPHANT

The Elephant is the symbol of strength, sagacity and prudence. Together with the Lion, Tiger and Leopard, the Elephant represent power. By lodging a stone on the back on an Elephant a childless women hope to have a male infant.

It is faithful and loyal to its server and may not serve another man.

The Elephant symbolizes the year. Its liver moves around its four legs according to the four seasons. It has twelve kinds of meat, corresponding to the twelve Zodiac Animals; with the trunk of its own meat. The Elephant is thus a celestial animal (Eberhard, 1968, p.263).

The Elephant is sacred in Buddhism where the animal is said to offer Buddha flowers. It was supposed to bear the wish-granting gem and sacred bowl of Buddha. The White Elephant is believed to be the incarnation of a future Buddha. It becomes the symbol of the Buddhist kings of Burma and Thailand.

AUSPICIOUS LEGENDS OF ELEPHANT

Hindu legends depict the world as carried on the back of the Elephant.

The Elephant is linked with several thunder legends. Emperor Shun used the Elephants to root up the ground and pull out trees. Shun lived at the thunder swamp. His son is an Elephant (Eberhard, 1968, p.258).

Apparently, its was Shun who introduced plowing and pottery. He lived in Elephant country and is also associated with the Raven.

Shun's half-brother Hsiang, who was evil, was also an Elephant and has some roles in controlling rains and was thus worshipped as an Elephant God of rains and fertility. In some versions, this Hsiang was also Shun's son and was killed by Shun. This Elephant God is quite reminiscent of the Indian God Ganesan who has an Elephant head.

The Bear or Monkey Dance of Yu is also said to be an Elephant Dance (Eberhard, 1968, pp.73-74).

THE LION

HISTORICAL BACKGROUND

The Lion is not native to China and yet the Chinese culture features this animal. The Lion was occasionally brought in as gifts to the Emperor. Its introduction into Chinese culture is said to be linked to the coming of Buddhism which features the Lion as the defender of its faith and Law. These Lion of Corea or Dog of Fu could be found guarding the fronts of Buddhist temples.

It is common but not as common as the more well-known Tiger in Chinese art and motifs. It is often depicted in murals and drawings playing with a ball, this signifies that the Lion may be regarded as a mythical creature like the dragon and Phoenix.

The Lion is not one of the Heraldic or Zodiacal Animals, neither is it one of the animals of the Twenty-Eight Constellations. It is only with a bit of imagination that the Lion could be associated with the Tiger (q.v.), the Heraldic Animal of the West and the Lion-Dog (the Pekinese Dog, q.v.).

In Chinese drawings, the Lion is not a fierce animal. It is drawn with beautiful curled manes amidst peony flowers, signifying its association with wealth, which the peony also symbolizes.

AUSPICIOUS MEANINGS OF LION

Lion statues are often seen guarding the premises on roofs or by the doors of most native buildings. These stone Lions have the menacing look and are supposed to be demon-scaring devices.

The Lion is the symbol of majestic strength, courage and fortitude. Among Christians it is the symbol of Christ and His resurrection. The Greek also placed them on steles of Greeks who died in battles. "Leon" is actually the departed Lion! Its symbol of the resurrection was based on the belief that the Lion's cub was born dead but was licked by its parents in three days to life or awaken to life by its parents' roar after three days. In Asia Minor it was the symbol of the sun. The winged Lion was one of the fabulous winged animals of Assyrian art (Whitticks, 1960, pp.211-212). Stone Lions similar to those of the Chinese stone Lions have been found in the ancient Middle East Hittite Empire (1750 to 1380BC) (Figure 39.1).

This emblem of valour, energy and associated military wisdom is also regarded as such by the Chinese thus the Lion emblems are embroidered onto clothes of military officials of the second grade.

The Lion is a popular and delightful animal symbol in Chinese culture:

A pair of Lions statues may be placed one on each side of the front door to guard the home against entry of evil. The pair may also be placed outside temples doors.

A pair of Lions playing with a ball is often another way of depicting the pair of dragons with the moon-pearl. The Lion and ball motif are also seen on porcelain. They symbolize good luck, blessings and protection against evil. The ball represents the sun, the dual egg symbol of *Yin-Yang* or even a precious stone. It is said that it is the male which plays with the ball while the female waits by the side with its young.

Figure 39.1 Chinese Lions Statues.
Symbol of majestic strength, courage and fortitude. Lion statues
are popular with the Chinese and could be placed as a pair out-
side the main doors of homes and temples.
Lion statues were also popular in the ancient Middle East where
they were often winged. Insert shows wingless Lions of the Hittite
Empire. Lions are not found in China. There may be a link be-
tween the ancient Hittites and Chinese. (See text)

AUSPICIOUS LEGENDS OF LION

There are not many tales about the Lion in Chinese culture, but there are some obscure legends about the Lion symbolized in the Lion Dance (Figure 39.2).

Figure 39.2: The Lion Dance.
Lion Dances are held to welcome the riches of the coming year to the premises.

THE LION DANCE

The most popular version of the symbolic Lion is the acrobatic dancing Lion enacted by two persons one holding the decorated bamboo-frame Lion head and the other the silk-cloth Lion tail. It may be accompanied by two persons acting as the jester-monk owners with fans in their hands and seen playing with the Lion. The Lion is often seen visiting the homes and even offices during the first two weeks of the Chinese New Year as a symbol of bringing in good luck and blessings, as well as chasing off evil. It would be accompanied by the beating of the drum and cymbals and the letting off of fire-crackers to scare away the evil spirit. The dance finishes when the Lion receives the *chai-ching* which consists of an *angpow* (red packet) attached with some vegetables (usually green lettuce) to a red thread hung from a pole.

Lion dances are often performed by Chinese *kungfu* groups who use the Lion dances to practise a number of *kungfu* stances and kicks. The Lion dance ceremony may also be performed on occasions of welcoming important personalities and opening of new businesses. Sometimes, more than one Lion would perform the luck-welcoming ceremony. If there are three Lions, they would represent the red-faced black-bearded Kwan Kung, the yellow Liu Pei and the black-faced, black-bearded Chang Fei of the Han Three Kingdoms period. On large occasions, the Lion dance may be accompanied by a rarer dragon dance where the long dragon puppet held by poles are manipulated by several persons.

The Kwan Kung Lion denotes righteousness and courage, the Liu Pei Lion bravery and kindness, the Chang Fei Lion fearlessness. The black Lion is the young fighting Lion bringing good luck. The flower-faced white beard Lion is older and is mature, wise, calm and peaceful.

There is also the Northern and Southern Lion. The former has a short mane with thick furry body. The later has no mane and a thin fur body and need a wider space for movements.

The modern Lion dance is said to originate in the Ching dynasty. The emperor dreamt that a strange looking creature saved his life. When the emperor described the animal to an advisor, the advisor told him the animal resembled the Lion of the West.

RHINOCEROS

There are two types of Rhinoceros, one with a single horn on its forehead and the other which has an additional smaller horn. The animal thrives in the hot climate. The known distribution of the animal in China as far back as the Yang-Shao culture indicates that the climate over north China had become cooler.

The animal, which is extinct in China today, is known from Shang oracle bones, which shows that the ancient Chinese regard the animal as a form of Ox. This is because the oracle bone character *Hsi* for Rhinoceros has the subcharacter *Niu* for Ox. The Chinese has another character *Ssu* which also means Rhinoceros. Even today, the Chinese call the animal *Hsi Niu* meaning a sworded-cow.

The Shang Rhinoceros appears to be a white or pale greyish-blue animal (Hsu and Ward, 1984, p.47).

Shang oracle bones records show that while it is difficult to catch the Tiger, Rhinoceroses were much easier to catch; as many as forty Rhinoceroses to one or two Tiger. The animal must have been plentiful during Shang times.

Up to the Warring States times, the tough and durable Rhino hide was used for helmet and armour which provided excellent protection against bronze (but not iron and steel) weapons. Such armours could last one to three hundred years. The hide had to be scraped, pounded and cut into pieces corresponding to the various parts of the armour (Hsu and Ward, 1984, p.166). The skin was also rarely used as an inner coffin layer (Eberhard, 1968, p.333)

The horn of the animal was, of course, very much sought after. As Dragon's Teeth they would be used for a wide range of medical purposes, including tonics and antidotes against poisons (Hsu and Ward, 1984, p.48) and as an aphrodisiac.

A pair of Rhinoceros horns symbolize happiness and is one of the Eight Treasures (Williams, 1931, p.306).

In legends connected with Emperor Ta Yu controlling the floods, the flood ch'iao dragon animal could be a Monkey, a Water-Bull or even a Rhinoceros (Eberhard, 1968, pp.60, 378-379).

SQUIRREL

The Squirrel is a common motif among decorative designs on embroideries and crafts.

The Squirrel with grapes symbolizes longevity (Burkhardt, 1982, p.206).

The Chinese do not have much to say about this animal, which therefore appears to have little significance.

THE FISH

HISTORICAL BACKGROUND

Fish was a staple diet of the early man living along the river banks of China. As more people moved inland, fish became a rarity and a delicacy, which was so by Mencius's times. The long coastline and the numerous rivers made fishing a popular occupation. Hence, a fisherman with his hat and bamboo fishing rod is a typical sight in Chinese paintings.

The Chinese eat a wide range of Fish. Fish is an important staple diet eaten with rice for the Chinese. But it is the decorative goldfish which fascinate the Chinese and feature in the ponds and fish tanks in Chinese homes. The Carp and Perch are often depicted in paintings and art pieces. The goldfish are favourite in painting motifs, often associated with luck. During the Yang-Shao period fish designs were common.

The so-called Dragon-Fish, the *Arrowana*, is a graceful species of the Carp and is an expensive collector item purported to symbolize abundant wealth.

The Carp is one of the few animals which, according to belief, could transform themselves into Dragons. When the Fish is one hundred years old it is ready to turn into a Dragon. Once the Carp leaps over the Dragon Gate it becomes a Dragon (Figure 42.1). Thus, symbolically, the Fish assumes several of the positive significance of *Lung*.

AUSPICIOUS MEANINGS OF FISH

In a Chinese banquet Fish is an essential dish. Where no Fish is available a symbolic wooden Fish would be part of the decoration (Hsu and Ward, 1984, p.52).

The Fish, especially goldfish, is a symbol of wealth and abundance, probably in recognition of its abundance in Chinese waters. An ability to Fish would prevent one from dying of starvation. The saying goes:

Give him a Fish today you have to give everyday; give him a fishing rod he will get his own Fish any day.

Figure 42.1: Carps leaping over Lung men (Dragon Gate).
Leaping across the Lung men, which is the cataract along the
Yellow River, signifies success in academic studies.
The ancient Chinese knew that literary success often means auto-
matic assurance of position and wealth.
(See Figure 5.6 for another illustration.)

Fish swimming in pairs signifies marital harmony and bliss. It is a good symbol to bless the newly married.

As such it is also used, in the goldfish form, as a charm to avert evil influences. Nine Fishes swimming gracefully signify abundance wealth. Temples often keep ponds or tanks of Tortoise and goldfishes, the latter to signify wealth and the former longevity.

In some temples, Fish statutes are found on rooftops to ward off fire. They also signify freedom from restriction and the freedom of the fully emancipated person. It is thus a holy emblem in Buddhism. Owing to its scaly armour-like skin, it is a symbol of military attributes especially martial valour.

The Carp is an ancient Chinese-Japanese symbol of endurance, perseverance, fortitude especially for young men and boys. This is particularly so in connection with efforts to pass literary examinations. Ancient legends claimed that letters had been found in Fish bellies.

A New Year wishing card with Carps jumping over the Dragon Gate is an auspicious symbol and common during this period.

During the third month of the year, along the Yellow River of China, the Carp would leap across cataracts and swim against the currents and rapids in order to reach the headwaters to spawn. These displays of courage and perseverance against the currents and obstacles to reach their goals are taught as a lesson to Chinese youth. The youth is encouraged to surmount all difficulties to achieve their goals and become human dragons. Japan adopted this symbol in the tenth century AD. where it featured in the Boys' Festivals on the fifth day of the fifth month known as the Feast of Flags. The Carp-shaped flags were attached to high bamboo poles. When the wind blows the cloth "carps" flap to simulate the Carp struggling against the current (Whittick, 1960, p.157)

The Carp is also auspicious for the reason that its name *Lei-Yu* in Chinese sounds like "Have Wealth". It is sought as a dish during the Chinese New Year to welcome luck into the house and one's life. The Chinese would eat the raw Carp as *Yee-Sang* during this period from the second day of the New Year. This dish is prepared from sliced raw flesh of the carp overlaid with spices, oil, sauce and wine. Everyone at the table will participate in the stirring the mixture to augur the good wishes for the New Year. This dish is more significant if taken on Everyman's Birthday, the seventh day of the Chinese New Year.

Fish was an early symbol of Christ and baptism during the first five centuries and appeared on sacrophagi, catacombs slabs, rings-lamps and architectural ornaments. It resembled the Dolphin, a pagan symbol. The initials of Jesus Christ is I X O Y E which is the Greek word for Fish. Three Fishes were often represented together as a symbol for the Trinity and which also gave rise to the *vesica piscis* the oval with pointed ends. The *vesica piscis* is found on panels as the sacred monogram. (Whittick, 1960, pp.183-185)

AUSPICIOUS FISH SAYINGS

Fishes were compared to the people and the ruler to the fishermen. Hence the art of government could be compared to angling. The bad ruler is a bad fishermen. The ancient Chinese believed that Fishes and birds could interchange with each other at appropriate times (Williams. 1931, pp.150-151)

There are a number of sayings depicting the tireless struggles of the Carp, especially in association with literary examinations:

- Fish becomes Dragon.
- Carp leaps the Dragon's Gate.
- Any man of ability can leap the Dragon Gate.

- Once scale the Dragon's Gate one's reputation increase ten-fold.
- Dragon leaps the celestial gate: Rise to a very high position.
- Bamboo sprouts shed their sheath; Fish tossed by waves will become dragons: No perfection without trials.

When the Carp has 300 scales it is in danger of being carried away by Dragons. Only the Tortoise could prevent this from happening.

The Carp is associated with the God of Literature who would be depicted riding on the back of the Fish-Dragon. This Star-God, Kuei, is often drawn as an ugly globin-like man with two crooked horn-like protrusions on his forehead.

The Chinese pragmatically realizes that suitable high education usually would bring automatic wealth. The educated man, with his refined mature dignity, is also respected and may even achieve great fame.

OYSTERS, MUSSELS AND SHELLFISH

The Oyster is well-known for the pearl it produces; but it is also a food delicacy. Mussels (Figure 46.1), another food delicacy, are said to be moon animals, being full during the full moon and empty during new moons.

The Cowrie shell, an ancient monetary item of exchange, is also a fertility symbol. The saying of "The old Oyster produces a pearl" refers to the child of an old man.

There is a belief that during fall and winter the Sparrows and Pheasants (or rather water-hens) would go into the water and turn into Mussels.

The Mussel is no ordinary Mussel but the sea-Mussel *Ch'en*. It is a large shellfish and when in charred condition it is used for funeral occasions. This is due to the belief that the Mussel is the proper food of the Earth God. Its use in funerals and tombs may also be due to the purifying effects of the lime in the shell (Eberhard, 1968, pp.291-292).

Mirages on the high seas are said to be caused by the *Ch'en* Mussel (Eberhard, 1968, p.293).

During the New Year period food dishes are selected according to the significance of that particular day. On the second day, the rooster is the principal dish. It may be served in combination with dace, mussels and oysters as the combination of names produces an auspicious motto for the coming year.

On the birthday of Tien-Hou on the twenty-third of the second Moon, vegetarian dishes are prepared. These dishes could include Oysters which are not credited with a soul. During the birthday of the Queen of Heaven, Tien-Hou, arches may depict the story of the Kingfisher pecking at the Oyster who clams its shell shut on the beak. Neither was willing to let go. So a fisherman came along and picked both of them into his net (Burkhardt, 1982, p.28). The politician Su Tai of the third and fourth centuries BC advised the King of Chao against the constant battles with the State of Yen. He gave the king the story of this Kingfisher and the Oyster (Williams, 1920, p.163). The moral is that one should not be involved in vain struggles.

SNAILS

Snail shells were among the various shells (including Mussel shells) which adorned the skeletons of many graves in Shang times (Waterbury, 1982, p.79).

In the story of the Heavenly Weaver Lady and her human Cowherd husband, the lady was also depicted as a Swan-Maiden or Snail-woman (Eberhard, 1968, pp.284-285).

There is a saying about Snails: "Where Snails trace characters on the walls and Swallows build their nests" – by the philosopher Huai Nan Tzu to describe a deserted house (Williams, 1920, p.203).

It is not known what the Snail signifies in Chinese culture. In Mayan art, the Snail signifies the Winter Solstice (Waterbury, 1982, pp.70-71).

THE FIVE POISONOUS ANIMALS

INTRODUCTION

The Chinese religious culture associates certain animals in groups. The more auspicious ones would be the Four Intelligents and the Four Supernatural Creatures (also described under other sections):

> The Four Intelligents or *Sze Ling* are *Lung* alias the Dragon; *Feng Huang* the Phoenix; *Lin* the Unicorn; and *Gui* the Tortoise. They are not superior to man. But these *Sze Ling* are believed to be endowed with special virtues for which they are respected and even venerated (Wu, 1982, p.5).

> The division of the celestial sphere into twenty-eight constellations was conceived more than 3,000 years ago, as it is mentioned in the Chou Ritual ... Seven of those stellar mansions were allocated to each of the four quadrants of heaven and were associated with four animals, often called the *Four Supernatural Creatures*. The Azure Dragon presides over the eastern quarter, the Vermilion Bird, i.e. the Chinese Phoenix – over the southern, the White Tiger over the western and the Black Warrior – i.e. the Tortoise – over the northern (Williams, 1931, p.336)

> The Heraldic Animals would become four or five *Lungs* or Bats, which are common good luck motifs.

Then, there are the Twelve Zodiacal Animals and the Twenty-Eight Constellations Animals, the latter composing of seven constellations under each of the Four Heraldic Animals. There are speculations that the Twelve Zodiacal Animals are a transformation of certain aspects of the Twenty-Eight Constellations Animals.

On the other hand, certain animals groupings, especially around the number five, were not so auspicious:

The Five Poisonous Animals are the Snake, Scorpion, Centipede, Frog and Lizard, having general symbolism of evil influences especially plagues and drought. A pot of Artemesia would be placed on the 5th day of the 5th month against them. Also, the demon queller Ching Kuei could be invoked in the last days of the fourth month as protection against them. His paper charms are pasted onto the rafters of houses. Another deity who could be invoked against these Five Poisonous Animals is Taoist Pope Chang Tao-Ling who rides the tiger on his excursions against evil, especially also on the fifth day of the fifth month (q.v. Tiger) (Plopper, 1935, pp.138, 186, 212).

It is curious to note that this fifth day of the fifth month is also the Dragon Boat Festival!

Another version of the Five Poisonous Animals is that they consist of the Viper, Scorpion, Centipede, Toad and Spider. Their combination has the power to ward off evil influences. Families with only one son would worship them. Often a picture of these five poisonous animals is embroidered in black silk on red cloth and the cloth are placed onto the clothes worn by the child on the first five days of the fifth Moon. Similar pictures are also found on some brass castings about two inches in diameter as charms against evil spirits (Williams, 1931, p.153)

These Five Poisonous Animals could be placed into a jar on the fifth Day of the fifth Moon. One of the animals would be left and used to make the *Ku* charm. Quite often the Snake would be left. This charm is a powerful love charm. It is also an evil charm which bring wealth to the owner through harming others. (for antidote, see Centipede).

Apart from these five poisonous animals there are also two groups of five animals which were explained in the previous chapters. They are the Five Great Families – Fox, Weasel, Hedgehog, Snake and Rat – and the Five Seers or *Wu Sheng* – Snake, Badger, Weasel, small Deer and Porcupine (Hedgehog).

There are also the evil spirits of Tiger, Wolf and Fox which could harm man. The Chinese thought that by worshipping them they could ward off the evil these very animals bring. Images of Tigers, Lizards, Snakes, Centipedes, etc., are used by the Chinese to help guard the children from colic and other infantile diseases. However, this concept may not be true to the ancient form.

Figure 44.1 illustrates a charm suspended from the roof on the fifth day of the fifth Moon and used against the Five Poisonous Animals. A flag with these animals painted is then stuck into a pot to serve as an additional protection against them.

This charm includes the Eight Diagrams or Pakua above the five animals. This Eight Diagrams itself is a charm symbol against evil influences. It is said that the power of the Eight Diagrams is invoked to work against the animals. The whole picture could give rise to the mistaken belief that the Five Poisonous Animals were being worshipped.

Likewise, when the images of these animals are placed onto paper or cloth which is red, the red is the actual a charm against the animals.

Figure 44.1: Paper Charm against evil influences of the Five Poisonous animals.
The charm is suspended from the roof on the fifth day of the fifth moon. The charm appears to spring from the invocation of the power of the Pakua. This fifth day of the fifth moon is also the Dragon Boat Festival and the time when the Taoist Pope Chang Tao-Ling rides out on his tiger to quell evil.

Tiger charms and sulphur are also believed to be able to protect one against these Five Poisonous Animals (Eberhard, 1968, p.158).

It is typical of Chinese animal symbolism that the auspiciousness attached to any particular animal is not necessarily entirely bad or good. The auspiciousness would depend on interactions with other influences.

Fundamentally, the inauspicious Five Poisonous Animals are actually the negation of the more positive auspicious Heraldic Animals.

THE FIVE POISONOUS ANIMALS

(See respective sections on Fox, Hedgehog (Porcupine), Snake and Rat)

Originally, the five animals are arranged in pairs of enemies representing day/fire/sun against night/ water/moon, plus the Frog (moon). On critical days the animals would fight each other and conclusions would be drawn from the results (Eberhard, 1968, p.161).

THE TOAD or FROG

The Chinese do not differentiate between the Toad and Frog which are common in wet areas like the rice fields. The tiny glistering jelly-like spawn of the Frog is regarded as the dew of heaven – hence the Frog is also called the heavenly chicken and used as an item for diet and medicine.

In Japan there was a story where the Frog claimed to have more knowledge than the gods. It is an ancestral spirit and guardian of the rice fields and rains in Indo-China. The Mongols believe the earth is supported by a Frog, reminiscent of Ceylonese legend that the earth rests on a giant Serpent lying on a Turtle held up by a Frog (Waterbury, 1952, p.7)

The Toad or Frog is linked to the Moon:

Yueh-lao the Chinese Old Man of the Moon is reputed to predestine and regulate the marriages of mortals. He ties the potential man and woman with an invisible cord which could never part so long as both are alive.

Another story is that the Chieftain Hou-I (or Feng-I), the famous inventor of arrows in the days of Yao-Shun and who shot down nine out of the ten suns, did not want to die. He thus obtained the black pearl of immortality from Hsi Wang Mu, the Queen Mother of the West. But his wife Chang-O inadvertently swallowed the pearl. She became immortal and light and floated away to the moon. Chang-O became the Frog on the moon. Hou-I was eventually reunited with Chang-O but Chang-O had to remain forever on the moon. The Toad outline is believed to be traced on the moon.

It is believed that there is a three legged Frog on the moon which swallow up the moon during an eclipse. It came to symbolize the unattainable.

The image of the Immortal Liu Hai with his three-legged Toad is considered the symbol of money-making. He is said to live during the Sung dynasty in the province of Shensi as the general who fought off the Nu-chen (Liu the Sea-Toad). Another version is that there was once the Toad which lived in a deep well and emitted poisonous vapours. Liu Hai lured the creature with a string of gold cash and destroyed it. During the local processions of the God of Wealth, Tau-Peh-Kong, the image of the three-legged Toad could be included in the procession along with the god.

The Immortal Chang Kou-Lao of the Eight Immortals is supposed to be the incarnation of the White Bat from before the Primeaval Chaos (q.v. Bat). He, holding a musical bamboo instrument, is often shown riding the white Donkey backwards but sometimes he rides this Toad.

THE SCORPION

The Scorpion is one of the Five Poisonous Animals – Snake, Frog, Centipede and Spider or Lizard – it is often replaced by the Spider.

The stings of Scorpions are warded off by placing willow branches and twigs on the head of the sufferer. (Burkhardt, 1982, p.16).

The significance of the constellation of Scorpio is similar to that of the Snake. Both symbolize evil. The constellation Scorpio has two opposite characters. It is either the good "Eagle" Scorpio which is generous, refined, reliable and astute, or the bad "Snake" Scorpio which is destructive, unreliable, deceitful, irrascible, calumniators and prevaricators (Joel, 1977, p.71).

Scorpion-men were guardians of the gates of the sun in Mesopotamia. In Hittites' symbolism, the Scorpion-men became Scorpion-Birds (Waterbury, 1952, pp.12-13).

The western astrology recognizes the southern constellation of Scorpio as either the biting Scorpion dying of its own poison in its struggle for survival or the noble Eagle which is the healer and magician who battles the forces of evil, darkness and triumph (Lutin, 1988, p.11).

Scorpio is thus the representation of conflict. It has three decans all symbolizing conflict (Seiss, 1972, p.18):

1. The Serpent with which Ophiuchus struggled.
2. Ophiuchus, struggling with the Serpent and being stung by the Scorpion also crushing the Scorpion.
3. Hercules holding the three-headed Snake or Dog of hell.

In reality the Scorpio constellation represents the noble Eagle destroying the evil Snake. The noble Eagle is also the *alter ego* of the Phoenix or Falcon which is symbolized by the winged disc or Eight Diagrams-Pakua. Hence the inclusion of the Eight Diagrams-Pakua on the charm of the Five Poisonous Animals.

THE LIZARD

The Lizard is one of the Five Poisonous Animals. The gecko or *shou-kung*, which is another name f Lizard, is a creature of the night and is the enemy of the Scorpion. It is supposed to eat the Scorpion.

The gecko is reared until it is about seven pounds. It is placed into a jar on the fifth Day of the fifth Moon and killed the following year. It is then smashed and made into pounded substance which is smeared onto the body of the virgin girl. The substance will be used during sexual union. It is supposed to prevent the girl from becoming immoral.

In Sumatra, the heads of deceased chiefs were placed in coffins ornamented with birds or Lizards. In Tahiti the Lizard, along with nature items like a stone, tree, or even snail, is considered to have a tutelary spirit. But for the Maoris and Easter Islander the Lizard represented the reptile ancestor (Waterbury, 1952, pp.42, 79, 136).

THE CENTIPEDE

Another member of the Fiver Poisonous Animals is The Centipede.

Along with the Rat, a red Spider, and Snake, the coming of a kind of northern Centipede into the house is a money-spinner sign (Burkhardt, 1982, pp.197-198).

Love charms made on the fifth Day of the fifth Moon are most effective. This love charm is called a *Ku* and is really a form of snake spirit. In order to work against this charm, the centipede, the *jang-ho* plant (a form of wild ginger) and the lotus root are used as antidotes individually or collectively. *Ku* magic can kill and a traveller who happens to carry a centipede with him is not harmed (Eberhardt, 1968, pp.151-152).

THE SPIDER

The Spider is another member of the Five Poisonous Animals, along with the Snake, Frog, Centipede and Scorpion.

It is a creature of the night as it weaves at night and often replaces the Scorpion (Eberhard, 1968, p.159).

It is also a money-spinner sign when it enters the house. (Burkhardt, 1982, pp.197-198).

THE WEASEL

The Weasel is one of the five calamity animals with the Fox, Hedgehog, Snake and Rat. Not much else is known of the Weasel.

INSECTS

Insects (Figure 45.1, 45.2) are common motifs on Chinese furniture, clothes, crafts and paintings. Some of the significance of insects are connected to the Ganzhi System – as explained the last chapter "Five Poisonous Animals" – and the Worms among the Twenty-Eight Constellations. Other significance are described below.

Fifth of March is the *Ching Che* Festival. *Ching Che* means "Arousing from Hibernation". It is also known as the Festival of Excited Insects where certain fetishes are placed out to placate the insects. This is also the day when images of the White Tiger is put up to keep away Rats, Snakes and to prevent quarrels.

ANT

The Chinese character for the Ant combines the meanings of righteousness and crawling things, describing their habits – hard-working, orderly and obedient.

It is a symbol of industry and resourcefulness. See Proverbs 6:6-9 in the Bible about the Ant:

> Go to the ant, thou sluggard; consider her ways and be wise: Which having no guide, overseer, or ruler, Provideth her meat in the summer and gathered her food in the harvest. How long wilt thou sleep, O sluggard?

It is also the emblem of virtue and patriotism and at the same time indicates self-interest, love for filthy money. The saying is "Ants come to what is rank smelling."

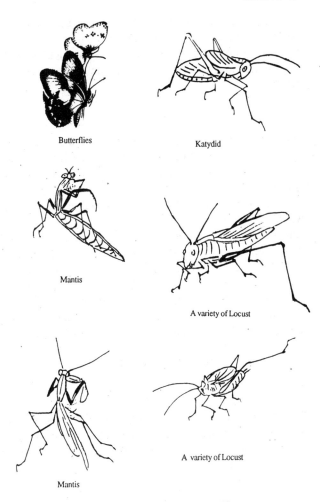

Butterflies

Katydid

Mantis

A variety of Locust

Mantis

A variety of Locust

Figure 45.1: Butterflies, Mantis and Locust.
Butterflies – symbol of summer and joy. Often associated with
Bats to signify abundant and joyful wealth.
Mantis – symbol of greed and pertinacity.
Locust – symbol of plague on crops.

The Chinese has long admired the organization shown by the Ant and the internal network of the Ant's nest. They themselves were compared by Westerners to the population of Ants; industrious and forever working away to make more money.

BEE

Bees are well-known for their honey, which is a delicacy and have additional medicinal value. The monks living in the mountain temples keep the Bee, *Apis mellifica*, to obtain honey.

A fortnight after the Festival of Excited Insects coincides with the blossoming of first flowering trees of sallow and the yellow willow. The nectar from these flowers served as food for the Butterflies and the Bees (Burkhardt, 1982, pp.13, 16).

The Chinese Bee is said to be of very gentle disposition. It is a symbol of industry and also ability and perseverance in stimulating growth and prosperity. It also symbolizes thrift.

A crowd of people is compared to a swarm of Bees while honey mixed with oil is a reference to false friendship.

BEETLE – See CICADA

THE BUTTERFLY

The delicate Butterfly is a favourite motif for the poets and painters. Owing to its intricate colourful designs on the wings, it demands great skill on embroiderer and painters of porcelain ware to bring out the best in them. It is the symbol of summer and joy.

The hibernating Butterflies usually come out about a fortnight after the Festival of Excited Insects to take advantage of the blossoms of the first flowering trees in spring.

The Butterfly conveys a wish for longevity and paper lanterns of Butterfly shapes may be presented with a wish that the recipient may live up to at least 70 or 80 years.

The Butterfly Cat, whose skin has blotched not striped markings, is considered lucky. Cat and Butterfly are often combined to convey the wishes for 80 to 90 years of life. Butterfly (*Tieh*) is for 70 to 80; while Cat (*Mao*) is for 80 to 90. Their combination is popular on jade pieces (Burkhardt, 1982, pp.195, 206).

It was said that the philosopher Chuang-Tzu dreamt that he was a Butterfly flirting happily among flowers and sipping nectar. When he awoke he was unsure whether he was human or a Butterfly. In another story a youth was chasing a Butterfly and entered unwittingly into the garden of a retired magistrate. He saw the beautiful daughter and determined to work hard to marry her. He was successful and rose to high rank.

THE CICADA

The Cicada is the insect which, during the summer, makes the stridulous and at times irritating sound to attract the females. It is not a Locust which is destructive to crops. Its main enemy is the Praying Mantis.

As it lives longer than other insects, the Cicada is the symbol of happiness and eternal youth. It is a common subject in Chinese painting.

The insect could be seen coming out from the ground after pupating for four years. Coming out from the grave grounds, the ancient Chinese see it as the symbol of immortality. Hence, a Jade Cicada would be placed in the mouth of the dead before burial.

The Cicada has similar significance to the Egyptian Scarab, another Beetle. The Scarab, an Egyptian species of Beetle named *Scarabaeus sacer*, is a symbol of life through creation and revival. This apparent power of recreation is linked to the female's habit of depositing its egg (which is protected in a ball) into a hole from which a new Beetle emerges. The Egyptians might have also compared the ball to the sun although the Egyptian often depicted the sun as a disk not a globe. Tiny images and statues made of porcelain and stone bearing the Beetle's symbols were used as amulets and seals. A larger kind of beetle was placed on the heart of the dead to protect the dead. They were also tokens of good fortune and good luck for which they were often used as seals to contracts (Whitticks, 1960, pp.251-252)

CRABS

The Crab is a delicious Chinese food item. They are also common themes in Chinese paintings.

Crabs are used in demon exorcism in Fukien. The priest would perform the ceremony to frighten off demons who would want to harm the unborn child inside the womb of the pregnant woman. He would recite the words and then burn several varieties of grass together with paper images of the Crabs. Sometimes several live Crabs would be released onto the streets to frighten off the spirits. It appears that one of the demons has a name that sound like the character for Crab. (Dennys, 1968, p.11)

CRICKET

The Cricket is associated with the autumn.

The common chirping Cricket is used for gambling. Two Crickets would be made to fight each other as the gamblers would bet on which would win. Before the fight the limbs of the insects would be torn off to prevent them from jumping away. Good fighters would be prized as pets.

The Cricket is also the emblem of courage and summer.

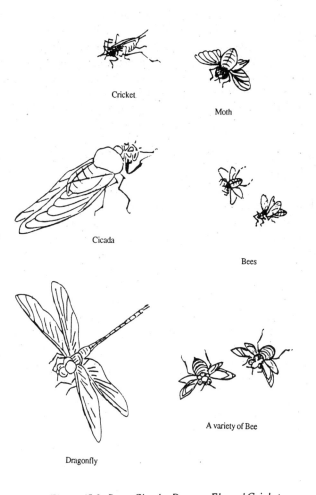

Cricket

Moth

Cicada

Bees

Dragonfly

A variety of Bee

Figure 45.2: Bees, Cicada, Dragon-Fly and Cricket.
Bees – symbol of industry, ability and perseverance;
Cicada – symbol of happiness and eternal youth;
Dragon-Fly – symbol of summer, instability and weakness;
Cricket – symbol of summer and courage.

Cheng, being stupid, often failed in his examinations. He was made a beadle to the Governor of Huayin and was told to collect Crickets for him. Cheng eventually ran out of money to buy Crickets and was at his wits end when he decided to commit suicide. His wife scolded him and asked why he had to killed himself when he could go out and search for the Crickets. He took the advice and went but only unimpressive specimens were caught and was later punished by the magistrate. Cheng's wife then sought the aid of a fortune-teller who gave her a picture to show where Cheng could catch good Crickets. Cheng then caught a good specimen by a temple which looked like the place indicated in the picture. But Cheng's nine-year-old son opened the bowl and the Cricket jumped off. The boy tried desperately to seize the Cricket but torn off one of its legs. The boy panicked and ran off. Later he became unconscious. At this time another Cricket appeared and was caught by Cheng. It had well-formed features but smaller then most crickets. He decided to test it to see whether it could fight. To his surprise the little Cricket began to win its bouts even against bigger opponents. It once managed to escape a cock's attempt to eat it and perched on the cock's comb. Cheng placed the Cricket in a small cage and presented it to the magistrate. The magistrate in disbelief astounded at the small Cricket's fighting feats and sent it to the Governor who in turn was surprised and sent it to the Emperor. The Emperor rewarded the Governor who in turn rewarded the magistrate who excused Cheng from his beadle's duty and instructed the Literary Chancellor to pass Cheng. A few months later his son regained consciousness and related his dream that he was a Cricket who proved to be a skilful fighter. Cheng was also rewarded by the Governor and became rich.

DRAGON-FLY

The Dragon-Fly, gracefully hovering above the flowers, is another common motif in Chinese painting and poetry.

The Dragon-Fly symbolizes the ninth Moon. During this time, paintings of chrysanthemums, water grasses and Dragon-Fly commemorate the noble but clumsy youth who was banished from the Imperial court (Bowie, 1911).

It symbolizes the summer and also instability and weaknesses.

It is also called the Typhoon-Fly as it seems to abound before storms. It is believed to be impregnated by the wind.

FIRE-FLY, GLOW-WORM AND LANTERN-FLY

The Fire-Fly, *Pyrophorus sp.* is not common in China. However, the Glow-worm, *Lampyris nocttiluca*, and the Lantern-Fly, *Fulgora candelaria*, are found in China.

Legend has it that Chu Yin of the Chin dynasty studied by the light of a bag of Glow-worms as he could not afford a lamp. He rose to high position in government. Thus, the Glow-worm is regarded as a sign of beauty, industry and perseverance. As it seems to regenerate from rotting vegetation, it is also an emblem of regeneration and the soul of the departed.

The Lantern Fly is a pretty green insect with a number of yellow bands around its body. It has a head with a drawn out snout that has a luminous tip.

GRASSHOPPER and PRAYING MANTIS

To the ancient Athenians the Grasshopper is a symbol of nobility reminding them that they are of a noble race and homebred. (Whitticks, 1960, p.193)

The Praying Mantis is a slender insect with a pair of front legs folded as if in prayers. It attacks other insects including those bigger than it like the Cicada. It is represents greed and pertinence.

LOCUST

The Locust is a serious pest in China and elsewhere. Ma Cha Shen, the Goddess of Locusts, was the divorced wife of Chiang T'ai Kung. She was later canonized into the honour and power of the office. The Goddess is worshipped by the farmers in the north where the locust is a plague. She is greatly feared because she can prevent or bring famine to the land as she chooses. Men do not seek her help but rather beg her to leave them alone:

Oh Locust Goddess! Oh Locust ruling powers!
Eat all our neighbour's crops, but don't harm ours.

The saying above is also a wish for harm to fall on others but not oneself (Plopper, 1935, p.177).

MOSQUITO

Mosquitoes are common in the south of the Yellow River and along the Yangtze Kiang in China. Mosquito nets, incense coils, and wire gauze window nets are measures used against them. In modern times we use DDT sprays onto water bodies to prevent the larvae from multiplying.

The Mosquito signifies wickedness and rebellion as below:

A multitude of evilly disposed people will stir up strife just as a crowd of Mosquitoes can make a noise like thunder.

PRAWN OR LOBSTER

The Chinese word *Ha* for Prawn or Lobster means mirth. The animal therefore symbolizes mirth or contentment in life.

BIRDS

INTRODUCTION

Birds are delightful colourful flying creatures and their flights grace the high heavens. As such, they often assume symbols of the gods of the skies. They are either the mascots and messengers of the gods or the very personifications of them. Their sounds tell Man a myriad of signals; of the onset of spring, of the approaching darkness or winter, and their silence means danger lurking about.

A wide variety of birds have been symbolized by the Chinese since ancient times. The ancient bronze symbols of birds could be grouped into four main types (Waterbury, 1952, pp.85-86):

I   With curving crest and long flowing tail, seems to represent the wind-deity and the *Feng Huang*.
II   Medium to small size birds of prey
III Larger birds of prey in upright pose, like the Falcon or Eagle
IV   Crestless birds like Doves and Ducks

These flying creatures generally do not chirp at nights. Unless they are night creatures like the Owl, the sound of a bird during the dark period from dusk to dawn would be inauspicious. Chirping of birds is especially prominent at dawns and dusks which are the periods of greatest activities. Strange behaviours of birds are indicative of omens which those who understand them may be able to take advantage in various ways.

There are so many of them. One of them is the association of birds with each month of the year. Every individual month is associated with specific birds (Bowie, 1911, pp.86-96) (Fig. 46.1):

- **First Moon** Associated with the New Year auspiciousness are the Stork and the Tortoise, both representing long life. The Stork lives for one thousand years and the Tortoise for ten thousand years. The pine is also the tree of this season and thus the Stork is often painted with the pine tree. The Falcon is associated with the seventh day of the New Year.

- **Second Moon** The Cock and Hen are the birds of this month. Plum and Chickens augur the period. The Cock's crow means "Happiness to our nation" and also "Eastern skies are reddening" – red being the lucky colour. It is the period of the last of the snow.

- **Third Moon** The peach apricot flowers are vogue this period, being the symbol of long life. No bird is auspiciously associated with this period. You may find the Crow denoting the end of spring.

- **Fourth Moon** Wistaria blossoms are out. The small bird "sudachi dori" is often painted on the wistaria branch. It reflects parental affection as the mother bird cares solicitously for its young.

- **Fifth Moon** The iris now blooms. The Cuckoo bird, the moon, the Carp leaping the waterfall are favourite symbols of this month. The fifth day of the fifth month is also the Japanese victory over Kublai Khan's fleet in the thirteenth century.

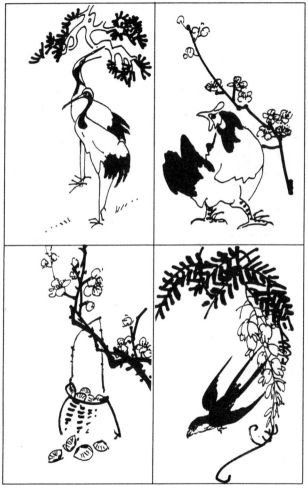

Figure 46.1: Birds and Flowers of the Seasons.
First Moon: Stork and Pine.
Second Moon: Hen and Peach.
Third Moon: Shellfish and Peach.
Fourth Moon: Swallow and Wistaria.

Figure 46.2: Birds and Flowers of the Seasons.
Fifth Moon: Cuckoo and Iris.
Sixth Moon: Golden Crow and Bamboo.
Seventh Moon: Kingfisher and Lotus.
Eight Moon: Sparrows and Rice.

Figure 46.3: Birds and Flowers of the Seasons.
Ninth Moon: Dragon-Fly and Arrowhead.
Tenth Moon: Geese over Marsh Grass.
Eleventh Moon: Duck and Chrysanthemum.
Twelfth Moon: Falcon and Pine, with Wren.

- **Sixth Moon** The cool feelings of the waterfall are depicted this month and bamboo pipes carrying waters suggest the coolness. A small bird would be bathing in the waters.

- **Seventh Moon** This period the birds all come out in colourful plumages to rival the colourful flowers.

- **Eighth Moon** Rabbit on the moon, sparrows on rice are favourite paintings of this month. The Rabbit is said to be making rice cakes on the moon. This is the moon worship period.

- **Ninth Moon** Chrysanthemums, water grasses and Dragon-Fly are painted. They commemorated the noble youth who was banished from the Imperial court.

- **Tenth Moon** The Geese come from the cold region and grace the sky with their flights. Monkeys and Squirrels also flighted among persimmon trees and look for mushroom. All these symbolize constancy.

- **Eleventh Moon** The last of the chrysanthemums cling to the bamboo fence and the first snow falls. The Dog enjoys this period. Mandarin Ducks (Fig. 46.4) during this period symbolize the maternal devotion and conjugal fidelity. It is a good time for weddings.

- **Twelfth Moon** White chrysanthemums blossom forth, the narcissus shows itself. The plum branch abounds with many small birds. The Falcon caught a bird in its claws but do not kill it. Letting it go, the Falcon would not hunt this bird for the next twenty-four hours. It is the time of nobleness.

While most of the birds in the Chinese tales are found naturally there are some mythical birds such as the Phoenix which is the most well-known. Others are:

- *Peng Niao* the Chinese Roc of enormous size and swift flight. It symbolizes rapid advancement in study and success in life.

- *T'ung Li* bird or *Yun Jih* bird. It is black and has a nine-inch neck and a voice ike a drum. It feasts on snakes. Wherever it roosts the plants below it would die. Wine seeped with its feather become very poisonous. The poison is known as the *chen* poison.

VARIOUS BIRDS

(q.v. also Phoenix in Heraldic Animals series, Cock-Hen in Zodiac Animals series and the Pheasant, Crow-Raven, Swallow in the Twenty-Eight Constellations series).

THE BULBUL

The Bulbul is a small bird with a white hoary head. It always fly in pairs. Hence, it is a symbol not only of longevity but also of the auspiciousness of a marriage where the couple would be together always even when their hairs have turned white like the hoary heads of the Bulbul.

Hence the Bulbul would be painted with peony flowers to signify both wealth and longevity and the painting makes a good present to the newly-wed. The pair of birds may also be painted with other foliages like the Malklow and the Camelia (Liang, 1979, p.153).

THE DOVE

Various species of Columbus, Doves and Pigeons are found in China including the Eastern Turtle-Dove, *Turtur orientalis*.

To the Chinese the Dove symbolizes long life while in other cultures, such as the Egyptians, it symbolizes innocence (Williams, 1931, p.108). To the Christians, the Dove is the symbol of the Holy Spirit and owing to its habit generally denotes innocence, gentleness, affection and constancy. The Dove with an olive branch in its beak symbolizes peace and glad tidings (Whitticks, 1960, pp.175-176).

During the Han dynasty, the Dove or Pigeon, supposed to be the messenger of Hsi Wang-Mu, Queen of Heaven, was adopted as a symbol and its image crowning a jadehandled staff was bestowed on a person's eightieth birthday . It was presented to old people with a wish that the old person would live long and able to digest food as the Pigeons do.

Like the Crane, the Turtle-Dove could also dance the Dance of Yu to lure out the Snakes and kill them (Eberhard, 1968, p.385).

The Chinese also regard the Dove as stupid and lascivious but faithful, impartial and filial. This is due to observations of the Dove feeding her young with marcerated food from its crop; the wood Pigeon feeds her seven young ones in one order in the morning and then the reverse in the evening.

Eating Dove eggs are said to prevent smallpox (Williams, 1931, p.108)

Using the rhyming of seven (*ch'i*) with one (*i*),the Book of Odes praise virtuous conduct:

> The turtle dove is in the mulberry tree
> And her young ones are seven in number
> And virtuous man, the princely one
> Is uniformly correct in his deportment.

THE DUCK

Besides the domesticated Ducks, the wild Ducks frequent the watery margins of several lakes in China. Hunters used to cover their heads with water gourds pierced with holes and waded into the waters. As the unwary Ducks would not be frightened off by floating rubbish, they could be approached very closed and pulled off from the water. They could also be caught with strings tied to bamboos placed at certain heights above the water to which hooks were attached and to which the birds would be impaled when they landed onto the waters. Modern hunting methods however use guns.

Figure 46.4: The Mandarin Ducks among Lotus.
The Mandarin Ducks are popular symbols of harmonious mar-
riages. They would be drawn with the Lotus to signify purity or
the Peony Flowers to signify wealth in marriage.

Ducks are common items of food. The Chinese believe that people recovering from skin diseases should not eat Duck flesh though the eggs could be taken. This is possibly due to the known dietary habit of the Ducks in looking for food among the mud.

In ancient times, feather dresses were made of Swan and Goose feathers. The fairies are said to wear such dresses. Later the term "feather dress" refers to the Taoist robe (Eberhard, 1968, p.285).

The Duck is an emblem of felicity. The Mandarin Duck, *Aix galericulata* or *Yuan yang* and *Hsi Ch'ih*, is a beautiful bird and is so-called on account of its superiority to the other ducks in beauty. The pair of the Mandarin Ducks are said to be very attached to each other and one would pine away if the other dies. The pair of Mandarin Ducks under the lotus are common motifs in Chinese paintings to symbolize marital happiness.

The Eleventh Moon is also symbolized by the Mandarin Ducks and is a good time for weddings (Bowie, 1911, pp.86-96). Some sayings connect the Duck with auspicious marriages:

The Mandarin Ducks make a couple: Wishes for the bridegroom and bride to be happy.

Separating the Mandarin ducks: To break up an engagement or to separate husband and wife.

It is said that when a man and his wife are well mated during life they would become Mandarin Ducks after death.

When one walks pass a Duck and the Duck quack it is considered unlucky. The lone quacking Duck is an ill omen. Quacking is done in a group and a lone quacking is therefore unusual and a bad sign.

The Duck and the Crane is associated with funerals rituals. On the sixtieth day after death, the family would place

various offerings of food, etc., on a table accompanied by the
burning of incense. A water bowl with some water in it is then
placed together with the offerings and in the water is a half
Duck egg with a bamboo Duck. A paper human image would
be placed there, too. The purpose was to personify the
provision of two alternative transports for the dead soul to the
nether world. He could either choose the shell boat or the
Duck itself. In place of the Duck, a paper sedan chair was
sometimes used. This was said to transport the dead soul to
Heaven using the Crane as the carrier (Dennys, 1968, pp.24-
25)

THE GOOSE

The Goose is regarded as the bird of *Yang* and embodies the
principle of light and male in nature. The Geese follow the
sun and migrate to the South in winter.

The wild Geese was formerly the emblem of the robes of
civil official of the third grades (Williams, 1931, p.180)

Geese were found in south China and in the north of the
Huai river, they were rare and expensive. Raising Geese was
considered to be women's work (Eberhard, 1968, p.286).

Geese always fly in pairs and were a symbol of marital
harmony as far back as the Chou times. They never mate a
second time. Hence the Chinese would pour a libation on the
Geese when the bridegroom fetches the bride from her
father's house (Williams, 1931, p.180). In some places the
bridegroom's family would send a male Goose while the
girl's family would in return give a female Goose. The bird is
thus a fertility symbol (Eberhard, 1968, p.286).

The tenth Moon is symbolized by the Goose. The Geese
come from the cold region and grace the sky with their flights.
Monkeys and squirrels also flighted among persimmon trees
and look for mushroom. Together they symbolize constancy
(Bowie, 1911, pp.86-96)

Once during the Han dynasty, Su Wu was detained by the Hsiung-Nu or Turks. He attached a letter to the leg of a wild Goose which was subsequently shot in the Imperial grounds. The note was eventually delivered and steps were taken to free Su Wu (Williams, 1931, p.180)

There is another fable about the good Geese trying to help the Tortoise (see Tortoise). This reflects the good nature of the bird:

> Two Geese were living with a Tortoise beside a pond. The hot weather came and dried up the pond. The Geese pitied the Tortoise and offered to take it to another place where there was water. They instructed the Tortoise to seize the middle of a stick with its mouth so that they could carry him via the stick. The Tortoise was warned not to speak. So off they went. The boys of the land saw them and shouted "See. Geese carrying a Tortoise!" Tortoise, irritated at the continual taunts, lost his temper and retorted. Alas, it fell down and was dashed to pieces (Dennys, 1968, p.149).

> Moral: avoid unsuitable agreements.

THE KINGFISHER

The Kingfisher, *Halcyon smyrnensis*, of the Alcyon family, builds its nest on water and is said to have the power to calm the waves.

The feather of the Kingfisher are used to make feather dresses. Being found in the south, the bird is sometimes sent as a tribute to the north. Its feathers are used for women's ornaments and until recently the bridal head ornament was made of alcyon feathers (Eberhard, 1968, p.287).

It is a beautiful bird. Its plumage had been used by the Chinese to inlaid onto silver or copper works. Head dress, combs, brooches, etc., were fashioned after the blues. The coloured pattern of the kingfisher were imitated on the tiny flowers and dragons. The artifact is not unlike the plumage of the Aztecs but they are not durable.

The Kingfisher is a popular emblem of beauty as its colours are said to vie with the sky and the tint of distant hills.

THE MAGPIE

The Magpie, *Pica caudata*, has a snowy white underpart, and is smaller than the Crow but just as noisy and mischievous and a nuisance to the peasants.

Headrests were made from Magpie's nests and from the small stones therein on the fifth Day of the fifth Moon. If the eggs salvaged from a burnt Magpie's nest on the fifth Day of the fifth Moon were fed to the sick they would recover (Eberhard, 1968, p.147).

The West has this saying of the magpies:

One for sorrow
Two for mirth
Three for a wedding
And four for a birth.

A solitary Magpie is a good omen to the Chinese. It is a *Yang* bird (but the Magpie is also called "divine maiden" or *Ku-chin-chu*) and its call is a good omen. The Chinese term for the bird is "bird of joy". A group of ten Magpies is also considered a good Chinese omen.

The chattering of Magpies indicates guests are coming to the house.

It is a symbol of marital fidelity (Eberhard, 1968, p.147). Magpies were featured in the legend of the Cowherd and the Heavenly Weaver Maid. They formed a bridge – The Bridge of the Magpies – once a year for the lovers to meet on the night of the seventh day of the seventh Moon – day of conjugal union. The Cowherd saw the Weaver Girl when she was bathing and both fell in love with one another. The Weaver Girl was the seventh daughter of the lord of Heaven. One version of the story said that the Lord of Heaven separated the lovers and allowed them to meet only once a year (Eberhard, 1968, pp.283-284; Williams, 1931, p.228)

The Magpie And The Birth Of The Manchus

The Manchurians arose to the north of Korea in the Long White Mountains between the forks of three rivers. In such cold climate where spirits abound there were three maidens. A Magpie dropped a red fruit on the robes of one of them. One of the maiden ate the fruit and became pregnant and bore a boy who could speak right away. But the mother died in the icy cave and the boy was placed onto a small boat in which he drifted. At that time, the three chieftains of the area were feuding and one of them went to the river and saw the boy in the boat. He believed that this was a good omen and chose the boy to head the fued settlement over the leadership. He adopted the title of Manchu. However, several generations later, in a revolt, the family was slain except Fan Cha-chin who fled to the desert. When he was pursued, a Magpie settled on his head and from the distance the enemies thought that he was a shriveled tree and passed him by (Williams, 1931, pp.228-229)

In another version, it is said that the Magpie dropped a fruit which cause a divine maiden to become pregnant and gave birth to the ancestors of the Manchus. The Manchus thus put up at funerals a pole with sacrificial meat for the Magpie (Eberhard, 1968, p.148).

THE OWLS

The Screech Owl, *Strix flammea*, and Horned Owl, *Otus vulgaris*, are found in China.

The Owl's natural food include Rats. In the tropics, they are favoured as a pest control animal where a breeding pair of Owls and their brood could consume 2,000 Rats a year. There are attempts to promote rearing of Barn Owls in estates. The bird is covered with mottled brown feathers which make it hard to be seen by its prey. It has a metre-wide wing span to help it to glide soundlessly. The eyes are big and can see well in the dark. It catches the Rat with its razor sharp talons. Likewise, it also hunts the Snake.

The Chinese dread the hooting of the Owl as it is a harbinger of death in the neighbourhood. It sounds like the expression for "digging the grave" in Chinese. There is a belief that when one is about to die the Owl would call out "dig, dig". It is also the bird which comes to take away the soul. Its voice is like the demon calling its fellow being.

The Owl, like the Frog, is a creature of darkness. The name *Hsiao* for Owl is the same Chinese character for killing a man and putting his head on a pole. The souls of the *Ku* magic are believed to be those who were killed in this fashion (Eberhard, 1968, p.155).

The Owl is considered an evil bird because the young are believed to eat their mother's eyes before they are able to fly; hence the Owl is blind. There is a saying that "The owl is an unfilial bird". Sons born on the fifth Day of the fifth Moon is like the Owl and would be unfilial to their fathers, whom they may kill. These sons have special powers which would be directed towards their fathers (Eberhard, 1968, pp.155, 159, 161).

The Owl is afraid of the Dog (Eberhard, 1968, p.162).

Taking broth of the Owl or Frog on the fifth day of the fifth moon, and taking a flower bath of iris or orchids, would protect one against the evil that comes on this day.

Traditionally the Owl was the creature of the Greek Athene and Roman Minerva the goddess of peace, learning, arts and wisdom. Hence the Owl is the symbol of wisdom even for the Christians. Moses rod was supposed to have a replica of an Owl on top of it (Whitticks, 1960, p.232). Some argued that that was not an Owl but a Hawk. The possibility of the replica being an Owl must not be ruled out because, like the Sparrowhawk (the Falcon), the Owl is also a bird of lightning and thunder. Owl statues were placed on tops of supporting columns and roofs up to the Han periods as protection against fire. (Waterbury, 1952, p.88).

In ancient bronzes, the Owl is depicted with a covering of animal decor and seems to reflect its status as a guardian of the ancestral spirits of the Shang rulers (Waterbury, 1952, p.87).

(q.v. Crow: Fable of Crows and Owls).

THE PARROT

The Parrot is mainly found in the south. The Parrot with its vivid colours is occasionally used as decorations on porcelains.

The Chinese had a legend that a pearl merchant who was nearly ruined by his wife learnt of his faithless wife activities from the house Parrot. Hence, the Parrot is a symbol to wives to be faithful to their husbands (Williams, 1931, p.275)

The Parrot is also the bird of the Goddess of Mercy, Kuan Yin, often perched on her side. It is believed to be a symbol of the Nimbus, or *Yin-Yang*.

THE PEACOCK

This beautiful bird, *Pavo mulicus*, is reared in many parts of China but it could be found only in the south.

It symbolizes beauty and dignity. Its feathers were used as decorations for meritious deeds. The Peacock with its spreading tail represents a congratulation message on the opening of a shop (Liang, 1979, p.3)

The Snake was said to be able to mate with the Peacock (Eberhard, 1968, p.385).

"Selection by hitting the bird screen" is the saying for the task of choosing a husband. The beautiful daughter of Tou I in AD562 painted a Peacock on a screen and offered to marry the man who could shoot the eyes twice in a row. The first Emperor of the Tang dynasty did that and was declared the successful suitor (Williams, 1931, p.278).

The Peacock is both a Christian and pagan symbol of immortality and the resurrection. The latter is due to the renewal of its beautiful plumage. The bird is sacred to Juno. As the Peacock kills Serpents it is also a Christian symbol against evil. It was only later that the Peacock was wrongly associated with pride through its beautiful appearance and love of display (Whitticks, 1960, p.236).

PELICAN

The Pelican with her youngs symbolizes Christ's work of redemption, sacrifice and also the resurrection. The analogy was that the Pelican used its own blood to nourish her youngs. The mother was supposed to kill the young with the fervour of her love but after three days the father would smite his side and pour his blood on the young who returned to life. This idea seems to be related to the secretion of blood from the Flamingo which ejected it from its mouth – the bird was confused with the Pelican (Whitticks, 1960, p.236).

THE QUAIL

The Quail, *Coturnix vulgaris*, closely associated with the partridge, is valued for its fighting qualities. The Chinese used them for Quail fights. Hence the Quail is a symbol of courage due to its pugnacious character. It is however also an emblem of poverty and patched clothing.

The Frog on the Moon is said to be able to change into a Quail, an emblem of the Sun (Eberhard, 1968, p.206).

SPARROW

Rabbit on the moon, Sparrows on rice are favourite subjects for paintings during the eight moon period. The Rabbit is said to be making rice cakes on the moon (Bowie, 1911, pp.86-96)

The Sparrow and the Pheasant are said to turn into mussels during fall and winter (Eberhard, 1968, p.290).

The Sparrow is one of the birds, along with wild Goose, Heron, Kingfisher, Pheasant, depicted as an escort during the funeral of a Japanese prince (Waterbury, 1952, p.61)

SWAN

The Swan has little Chinese significance.

The bones of other birds like fowl or heather-cock were found to belong to the Bronze Age. But it was the Swan which received early symbolism as the sun. In Siberia, the Swan is grouped under birds like Eagle, Vulture and Raven and they all have been regarded as the abodes of divine spirits. The Swan or Stork is supposed to bring children (Waterbury, 1952, pp.37, 63, 146).

The White Swan is the symbol of the male and female virgin and reflects beauty, purity and grace. (Whitticks, 1960, p.269)

THE FALCON

Introduction
When the Falcon soars to the sky, all flying creatures freeze. They are paralysed with fear. Small birds could be found shivering among the bushes and could be easily caught. Only

the Wren dares to shake its fear and flies like a bolt to escape the Falcon. The Falcon would sweep close to catch it but let it go in recognition of its courage.

This fear is also felt by the Eagle at the sight of the swiftly approaching Falcon. The Eagle is purportedly to be stronger than the Falcon but lacks its boldness. It may turn tail and flee. If the Eagle, recovering its courage and emboldened by its large size, chooses to meet the Falcon, there would be a fight in which both birds would be seriously injured.

The Falcon, majestic in form and courage, is the favoured hunting bird of kings, even in ancient China. The Peregine Falcon is a particularly striking bird in Chinese paintings.

The Chinese include the Eagles, Falcons and raptorial birds by the term *Ying* which is the symbol of one bird swooping down on another (Williams, 1931, p.141).

Auspicious Meanings of Falcon
The Falcon is among the predatory birds popular as ornamental images on furnitures and art pieces. It symbolizes boldness and keen vision. In feudal age, Falcon-banners styled Yu were borne in the chariots of higher chieftains as the symbol of authority (Williams, 1931, p.141).

It is associated with the First Moon, along with the Stork and the Tortoise both representing long life, and also the Seventh day of the New Year (Bowie, 1911, pp.86-96). It is also closely associated with the Twelfth Moon where the Falcon would catch a bird in its claws but would not kill it. It would let it go, and would not hunt this bird for the next twenty four hours. This is the time of nobleness.

The tail is supposed to be a curative charm against smallpox (Williams, 1931, p.141)

Link of Falcon with Phoenix
(See page 45 for more information) The Arabian Phoenix is a kind of Eagle (Williams, 1931, p.286). The sphinx was a common Egyptian symbol of power and there were three main types of these sphinxes, each with a Lion's resting body (Whittiocks, 1960, pp.263-265):

- Androsphinx, with a Man's head
- Hieracosphinx, with a Falcon's head
- Criosphinx, with a Ram's head

It is evident the Hieracosphinx, with its Falcon's head, is a version of the Phoenix.

Enigma of the Falcon
The Falcon may hold a clue to the ancient origins of the Chinese civilization. There is a close link between the Chinese circle symbol of the Eight Diagrams or *Pakua* and the Middle East symbolization of the Falcon:

> The Falcon or Sparrowhawk is the symbol of Horus and may take the form of the huge winged disk. Horus in this winged disk form would also take Nekhebit and Uazit the goddesses of the South and North in their Snake forms (hence two serpents). After Horus defeated the enemies of Ra, Ra was supposed to have told Thoth to place the image of the winged disk in the sanctuaries to banish evil from the vicinity.

> In the Middle Kingdom in Egypt this winged disk appears over entrances of temples, tombs, etc. and on top of stele to signify protection from harm. This winged disk is also the symbol of thunder, lightning and rains, the destructive powers of the gods against their enemies. The disk may appear by itself or it may have the two serpents attached to it on each side.

It symbolizes not only protection of life but also speed (Whitticks, 1960, pp.171-173).

Comments: This may be the reason why the wand of Hermes composes a cross of two Serpents with two wings at the top. As the Falcon is considered a natural enemy of the Snakes, it is possible that the winged disk as the symbol of the Falcon depicts its victory over them and thus carrying the two Serpents – likened to the symbol of the Eagle with its talons gripping the serpent. Thus in the double-Snake symbol of Asclepius, the god of medicine, it is not the Snakes which signify the healing power but rather the winged Falcon who is not fully shown but merely symbolized as wings or a knob on top of the wand of Asclepius.

Other Reference: The fleur-de-lis, the renderation of three white lilies, the symbol of life and its renewal is the sign of Horus. The fleur-de-lis is found to be the thunder-lightning weapon of Horus being associated with the lily (Whitticks, 1960, p.187).

The thunderbolt was the weapon of Zeus and was manifested as lightning indicating his wrath. The earliest symbol of the thunderbolt was a zigzag two-pronged or three-pronged fork, the former being probably earlier as seen in Mesopotamia in twelfth century BC. In ninth century in Assyria the thunderbolt was three-pronged fork. By the time it reached Greece the thunderbolt was represented by the lily (Whitticks, 1960, p.274). Therefore, it is possible the thunderbolt is the real nature of the trident!

Thus the Chinese Eight-Diagrams or *Pakua* has close kinship with the Falcon and its Middle East's symbol of the Winged Disc of Heaven! Like the Egyptian winged disc, the Chinese Eight Diagrams-*Pakua* is also a symbol used to ward off evil. The Falcon sweeping down against the Snakes in the wands of Hermes and Ascelpius really correspond to the

Chinese Phoenix in the South poised above the Black Snake down to the North!

There are reasons to believe that the Chinese race may be anciently linked to the Hittites of the Middle East:

The two Eagles in Chinese symbolism also appeared as far back as in the Hittites empire (Whitticks, 1960, pp.177-179).

The Falcon is said to be a Chinese emblem on its ancient war-chariots. The Chinese has been said to be the first culture to use the horse as a war animal (q.v. section on Horse). The Hittites were the first Middle East power to use the horse-drawn war-chariots around 1750BC. The Hittites had swept into Egypt, then into Babylonia and Assyria and further east to the Near East ... they would have continued east towards the Chinese nation.

In feudal age, Falcon-banners styled Yu were borne in the chariots of higher chieftains as the symbol of authority. There are archaeological relics of the Hittite empire depicting the banner of their chieftain. The banner composes of a circle with a pair of wings from its side – this is similar to the winged disc representing the Falcon of the Egyptian myth – however, one Hittite symbol has a Eight Points Star in the circle – very reminiscent of the Chinese Eight Diagrams or *Pakua*! In fact, a mother of pearly plague from An-yang (Shang dynasty 1400BC) has a star, with a well-defined center encircled by a narrow band and its eight petal-like points (Waterbury 1952, p.97).

THE STORK

Introduction

The Stork (or Crane or Heron), *Grus montignesia* or Manchurian crane, is a creature of the swamps. It is a popular bird in Chinese mythology and art, where it is often considered the alter ego of the Phoenix. There are four types, namely, the black, yellow, white and blue Cranes, of which the black ones are supposed to live the longest (Williams, 1931, p.84)

The Stork is the patriarch of the feathered animals and the special carrier of the Immortals, especially the God of Longevity and also Hsi Wang-Mu, the Queen of Heaven (Burkhardt, 1982, p.174).

King Mu was offered the blood of Cranes to prolong his life and he also saw the crane dance, which Huang-Ti was also reputed to see (Eberhard, 1968, p.65).

Auspicious Meanings of Stork

The Crane, like the fire, is regarded as an animal of the *Yang*. By performing the Dance of Yu, which is said to be a one leg dance, the Crane (also Dove) is said to be able to draw out snakes to kill them (Eberhard, 1968, pp.65-66). Feathers of the Crane could drive away or exorcise Snakes (Eberhard, 1968, pp.128,299).

The fire-Crane, the *Pi-fang*, is said to be the companion of Hui-Lu the Fire God. If it calls ten nights in a row it is a bad omen, which is occurred when the Hsia dynasty ended (Eberhard, 1982, p.66).

The Stork, supposing to live up to one thousand years, is one of the commonest emblems of longevity. When it reaches 600 years it does not take any solid food except drinks (Williams, 1931, p.84). It is often drawn with the pine tree to symbolize longevity and such drawings make good gifts of wishes for long life.

Human beings skilled in the black arts are supposed, after a thousand years, to be able to turn themselves in black Cranes and fly about (Williams, 1931, p.84). Sop, Taoists may compare themselves to Cranes (Burkhardt, 1982, p.65). It is also regarded as the companion of all pious Taoists who after mastering the secrets of the arts would enter into the Heavens riding its back (Eberhard, 1971, p.213).

The Stork symbolizes parental care, filial piety and affection. Hebrew for Stork is *hasidah* which also means "pious". The Romans engraved the stork onto medals of princes who earned the title "Pius". It was once erroneously thought that the bird would peck its young till they were killed and then healed by licking them. The Stork with a cradle in its beak is a symbol on christening cakes and denotes the idea of good parenthood (Whitticks, 1960, p.266)

The White Stork was the emblem of the officials of the fourth grade (Williams, 1931, p.84)

The figure of the Crane is sometimes placed on the centre of the coffin to symbolize the provision of a carrier to carry the soul to Heaven. The soul would be riding on its back to the "Western Heavens". The Crane, like the Deer, escorts the soul to immortality (Burkhardt, 1982, p.206; Williams, 1931, p.84).

After a funeral, the roasted meat may be carved up and distributed to guests in white paper. On this paper there is an image of the Manchurian Crane carrying a string of cash with two peaches below it. One inscribed with "Long Life" and the other with "Money". The bird may also grace the entrance on the mourning annexe (Burkhardt, 1982. pp.104-105).

EAGLE

The Eagle is the symbol of victory. It is a Christian symbol of the ascension. The Eagle was sacred to Zeus. Its talons gripping the serpent represents the triumph over evil and the victory of goodness. The talons sometimes hold the thunderbolt, the weapon of Zeus. It is sacred to the Roman Jupiter and is thus the standard of the Roman legions. The two Eagles also appeared as far back as in the Hittites (Whitticks, 1960, pp.177-179)

See also Hawk

HAWK

The Sparrowhawk or Falcon is the symbol of many Egyptian gods associated with the power of the sun. Horus is a Hawk-headed man with Hawk wings. Ra was represented as a man with a Hawk head surmounted by the solar disk and the Uraeus Serpent. It is also associated with Apollo the Greek sun-god. It is selected as the sun symbol in the belief that it could stare directly into the sun. It is thus regarded as filled with sunlight and as the bird of fire (Whitticks, 1960, p.196)

See also Falcon

BIBLIOGRAPHY

Bilsky, Lewster James. *1975. The Ancient State Religion Of Ancient China I.* Asian Folklore And Social Life Monograph. Lou Tsu-k'uang, Editor. Volume 70. The Orient Cultural Service. 422 Fulin Road, Shihlin, Taipei, Taiwan, China.

Bowie, Henry P. 1952. *On The Laws Of Japanese Painting.* Dover Publications, Inc. New York.

Bullinger Publication Trust. 1964. *The Companion Bible.* Zondervan Bible Publishers. Grand Rapids, Michigan.

Burkhardt, VR. 1982. *Chinese Creeds And Customs.* A SCMP Publication. Hong Kong.

Buttrick, George Arthur. Commentary Editor. 1954. *The Interpreter's Bible.* A Commentary In Twelve Volumes. Abingdon Press. Nashville, New York.

Chang, KC. *Art, Myth And Ritual: The Path To Political Authority In Ancient China.* Harvard University Press. Cambridge, Massachusetts and London.

Chavannes, E. 1973. *Five Happiness.* Weatherhill. New York, Tokyo.

Cheu, Hock Tong. 1988. *The Nine Emperor Gods: A Study Of Chinese Spirit-Medium Cults.* Times Book International. Singapore, Kuala Lumpur.

Denny, Nicholas, B. 1968. *The Folklore Of China And Its Affinity With The Aryan And Semitic Races.* Oriental Press. Amsterdam, Netherlands.

Derk Bodde, Translator. 1965. *Annual Customs And Festivals In Peking.* By Tun Li-Chun, 1900. Hong Kong University Press. Hongkong.

Eberhard, W. 1968. *The Local Cultures Of South And East China.* E.J. Brill. Leiden.

Eberhard, W. 1972. *Chinese Festivals.* The Orient Cultural Service. Taipei, Taiwan, China.

Fleming, Kenneth C. 1981. *God's Voice In The Stars.* Loizeaux Brothers. Neptune, New Jersey.

Huang, Tsai-Kang. 1986. *The Traditional Art Of Chinese Woodblock Prints.* Council For Cultural Planning And Development. People's Republic Of China.

Hsu, CH and Ward, AHC. 1984. *Ancient Chinese Society: An Epigraphical And Archaeological Interpretation.* Yee Wan Publishing Company, San Francisco, California.

Joel, C Dobin, Rabbi. 1977. *The Astrological Secrets Of The Hebrew Sages.* Inner Traditions International Ltd. New York.

de Kermadec, Jean-Michel Huon. 1983. *The Way To Chinese Astrology: The Four Pillars Of Destiny.* Translated by N. Derek Poulsen.Unwin Paperbacks, London.

Kwok Man-Ho. 1989. *The Chinese Almanac 1990: The Year of the Horse.* Bantam Books. Toronto, New York, London, Sydney, Auckland.

Lagerway, John. 1967. *Taoist Ritual In Chinese Society And History.* MacMillan Publishing Company. New York.

Lai Kuan Fook. 1984. *The Hennessy Book Of Chinese Festivals.* Heinemann Educational Books (Asia) Ltd. Petaling Jaya, Malaysia.

Lee Siow Mong. 1986. *Spectrum Of Chinese Culture.* Pelanduk Publications. Petaling Jaya, Malaysia.

Levi, Eliphas. 1825. *The Key Of The Mysteries.* Translated from French by Aleister Crowley, 1959. Rider, London, Melbourne, Auckland and Johannesburg.

Liang, Yin-Boone. 1979. *Chinese Flower And Bird Painting.* Wan Li Book Company Ltd. Hong Kong.

Low, CC, And Associates. (Editors And Translators) 1989. *Canonisation Of Deities.* Canfonian Pte Ltd. Singapore.

Lutin, Michael. 1988. *1988 Total Horoscope: Scorpio.* Jove Books, New York.

MacKenzie, DA. 1926. *The Migration Of Symbols.* AMS Press. New York.

Maspero, Henry. 1945. *Taoism And Chinese Religion.* Translated by Frank A Kierman Jr. 1981. The University Of Massachusetts Press. Amherst.

Needham, Joseph. 1959. *Astronomy.* Volume 3 of Science And Civilisation In China. University Press, Cambridge, Britain.

Peloubet, Rev F N. 1947. *Peloubet Bible Dictionary.* The John C. Winsten Company. Great Britain.

Plopper, Clifford H. 1935. *Chinese Religion Seen Through The Proverbs.* Shanghai Modern Publishing House, Shanghai, China.

Saso, Michael. 1978. *The Teaching Of Taoist Master Chuang.* Yale University Press, New Haven and London.

Seiss, Jospeh A. 1972. *The Gospel In The Stars.* Kregel Publications, Grand Rapids, Michigan.

Sharf, A. 1876. *The Universe Of Shabbetai Donnolo.* Aris & Phillips Ltd. Warminster, England.

Shumaker, Wayne. 1972. *The Occult Sciences In The Renaissance: A Study In Intellectual Patterns.* University Of California Press, Berkeley, Los Angeles, London.

Skinner, Stephen. 1982. *The Living Earth Manual Of Feng Shui.* Graham Brash (Pte) Ltd. Singapore.

Tun, Li-Chun. 1900. *Annual Customs And Festivals In Peking.* Translated by Derk Bodde. Hon Kong University Press. Hong Kong.

Vaccari, O and EE. 1950. *Pictorial Chinese-Japanese Characters A New And Fascinating Method To Learn Ideograms.* Vaccari's Language Institute, Tokyo.

Waterbury, F. 1952. *Bird-Deities In China.* Artibus Asiae Publishers. Ascona, Switzerland.

Weiger, LSJ. 1950. *Chinese Characters: Their Origin, Etymology, History, Classification and Significance. A Thorough*

Study From Chinese Documents. Dover Publications Inc., New York.

Whittick, Arnold. 1960. *Symbols, Signs And Their Meanings*. Leonard Hill Ltd. London.

Williams, CAS. 1920. *Manual Of Chinese Metaphors*. AMS Press. New York.

Williams, CAS. 1931. *Outlines Of Chinese Symbolism*. Customs College Press, Peiping, China.

Wing, RL. 1982. *The Illustrated I Ching*. Doubleday Dolphin Book.

Wong, CS. 1967. *A Cycle Of Chinese Festivals*. Malaysia Publishing House Ltd. Singapore.

Wu, Cheng Eu. 1500-82, Ming Dynasty. *Journey To The West*. Translated by W.J.F. Jenner. Foreign Languages Press, Peiking.

Wu, Kuo Cheng. 1982. *The Chinese Heritage*. Crown Publishers, Inc. New York.

Xing, Qi. 1988. *Folk Customs At Traditional Chinese Festivities*. Foreign Languages Press. Beijing.